ENCYCLOPAEDIA OF
INDIAN GOVERNMENT:
PROGRAMMES AND POLICIES

ENCYCLOPAEDIA
OF
INDIAN GOVERNMENT:
PROGRAMMES AND POLICIES

Vol. 21

Parliamentary Affairs and Democracy

Edited by

Satish Tiwari

ANMOL PUBLICATIONS PVT. LTD.

NEW DELHI - 110 002 (INDIA)

ANMOL PUBLICATIONS PVT. LTD.
4374/4B, Ansari Road, Daryaganj
New Delhi - 110 002

Encyclopaedia of Indian Government: Programmes and Policies

First Edition, 2000

ISBN 81-261-0515-1 (Set)

PRINTED IN INDIA

Published by J.L. Kumar for Anmol Publications Pvt. Ltd., New Delhi - 110 002 and Printed at Mehra Offset Press, Delhi.

Contents

Preface

Encyclopaedia of Indian Government: Programmes and Policies contains authoritative information on about fifty departmental policies and their future developmental programmes.

Organised to be completed in 40 volumes, this gigantic work covers Agriculture; Atomic Energy; Chemicals and Fertilizers; Coal; Commerce; Communication; Culture; Defence; Education; Environment and Forests; External Affairs; Finance; Food & Consumer Affairs; Food Processing Industries; Health and Family Welfare; Home Affairs and Internal Security; Human Resources; Industry; Information and Broadcasting; Labour; Law, Justice and Company Affairs; Non-conventional Energy Sources; Ocean Development; Parliamentary Affairs; Personnel, Public Grievances and Pensions; Petroleum and Natural Gas; Planning and Programme Implementation; Planning and Statistics; Posts and Telegraphs; Power; Rural Development; Science and Technology; Social Justice and Empowerment; Space; States Affairs; Steel; Steel and Mines; Sugar and Edible Oils; Surface Transport; Textiles; Tourism; Urban Development; Water Resources; Women and Child development etc.

Based on the information derived from authoritative sources, this work contains authentic facts and figures. I am deeply beholden to all the scholars whose writings are cited or substantially made use of in the present work. I am also thankful to Anmol Publications Pvt. Ltd. for undertaking publication of this encyclopaedia. I am solely responsible for shortcomings in presentation of matter.

Encyclopaedic in nature, this will prove a dependable reference work for scholars and academics besides those appearing for different competitive examinations.

—**Satish Tiwari**

1

Introduction

In a Parliamentary form of Government, the day-to-day working of the Parliamentary system makes large claims on time and resources of the various Ministries/ Departments. Over a period of time, Parliamentary programme covers numerous intricate matters-financial legislative and non-legislative-concerning various Ministries/Departments of the Government. The Ministry of Parliamentary Affairs, though small in size, is one of the key Ministries of the Union Government.

The task of efficiently handling diverse and enormous parliamentary work on behalf of the Government in the Parliament has been assigned to the Ministry of Parliamentary Affairs. As such, the Ministry of Parliamentary Affairs serves as an important link between the two Houses of Parliament and the Government in respect of Government Business in Parliament. Created in. May, 1949 as a Department entrusted mainly with the above function, it is now a full-fledged Ministry.

The Ministry renders secretarial assistance to the Cabinet Committee on Parliamentary Affairs, which, inter-alia recommends summoning of both the Houses of the Parliament and their prorogation.

The Ministry keeps a close contact with the Ministries/Departments of the Government in respect of Bills pending in the Parliament, new Bills to be introduced and Bills to replace Ordinances. The Ministry keeps a watch over the progress of Bills from the stage of approval by the Cabinet till the Bill is passed by both Houses of the Parliament.

In order to ensure smooth passage of Bill in Parliament, officials of the Ministry have to be in constant touch with the officials of Ministries/ Departments sponsoring the Bills and the Ministry of Law, Justice and Company Affairs who drafts the Bill.

The Ministry constitutes Consultative Committees of Members of Parliament and makes arrangements for holding their meetings both during the session and the inter-session periods. At present, there are 29 such Committees attached to various Ministries which were required to hold about 177 meetings in a year. The guidelines regarding the composition and functioning of these Committees are formulated by this Ministry. Notifications in respect of any Sub-Committees/Study Groups to be set up by the Consultative Committees are also issued by this Ministry.

The Ministry pursues with the other Ministries for prompt and proper implementation of assurances given by Ministers in the Parliament. There are also several other items of work allocated to this Ministry which involve liaison between Members of Parliament, two Secretariats of Parliament and the various Ministries. Looking after the welfare and amenities of the Members is also an important function assigned to this Ministry. The Minister of Parliamentary Affairs nominates Members on various Committees, Councils, Boards and Commissions set up by the Government. The Ministry also administers the Salaries and Allowances of Officers of Parliament Act.

1953, the Salary, Allowances and Pension of Members of Parliament Act, 1954, the Salary and Allowances of Leaders of Opposition in Parliament Act 1977 and the Leaders and Chief Whips of Recognised Parties and Groups in Parliament (Facilities) Act, 1998.

With a view to strengthening the roots of democracy and inculcating habits of discipline and tolerance and for enabling the student community Parliament, the Ministry conducts Youth Parliament Competitions amongst students of schools in the Government of National Capital Territory of Delhi as well as under the Kendriya Vidyalayas Sangathan all over the country.

As a part of celebration of Golden Jubilee year of India's Independence, the Vidyalayas of Navodaya Vidyalayas Samiti have been included for the first time in the scheme of National Youth Parliament Competitions on the pattern of Kendriya Vidyalayas and a scheme of Youth Parliament was also launched for the first time in Universities/Colleges all over the countries in cooperation with University Grants Commission and Association of Indian Universities ,during 1997-98.

The Ministry has also been conducting Parliamentary Quiz Competitions among students of Senior Secondary Schools and Colleges on Parliamentary Procedures, Constitutional provisions and the history of the freedom movement. Parliamentarians in any country contribute to the shapping of foreign policy and relations with other countries.

Particularly in the present international scenario, it is necessary and useful for the Government of India to chose certain members of Parliament and utilize their services effectively for winning over their counterparts in other countries to our side by explaining our policies, achievements and problems in various areas. With these objectives in view, the Ministry sponsors the delegations of Members of Parliament to other countries and also organises; the visits of Government sponsored Parliamentary Delegations from other countries to India.

Organisational setup

Shri Madan Lal Khurana, relinquished the charge of the Minister of Parliamentary Affairs on 30.1.99. Sh. P. R. Kumaramangalam, the Minister of Power, was entrusted the additional charge of the office of the Minister of Parliamentary Affairs w.e.f. 30.1.1999. Shri R.K. Kumar relinquished office of the Minister of State with effect from 22nd May, 1998.

Shri Dilip Ray, Minister of State (Independent Charge) of the Ministry of Coal, assumed the additional charge of the office of the Minister of State in the Ministry of Parliamentary Affairs with effect from 22nd May, 1998. Shri Ram Naik continues to be the Minister of State in the Ministry of Parliamentary Affairs with effect from 19.3.1998. On the administrative side, Ministry is headed by a Secretary to the Government of India who is assisted by one Joint Secretary, three Deputy Secretaries and six under Secretaries.

2

Summoning and Prorogation of Parliament Houses

Dissolution of eleventh lok sabha

The Eleventh Lok Sabha which was constituted on 15 May, 1996 was dissolved by the President on 4 December, 1997.

Constitution of twelfth lok sabha

The Election Commission constituted the Twelfth Lok Sabha on 10 March, 1998.

Summoning and prorogation of both houses of parliament

Article 85(l) of the Constitution empowers the President to summon each House of Parliament to meet at such time and place as he thinks fit. Clause (2) thereof states that the President may from time to time prorogue the Houses or either House or dissolve the House of the People (Lok Sabha). The Allocation of Business Rules framed under Article 77(3) of the Constitution assign this function to the Ministry of Parliamentary Affairs.

After assessing the time likely to be required for transaction of Government Business and for discussion on topics of public interest as may be demanded from time to time by Members of Parliament, a note is placed before the Cabinet Committee on Parliamentary Affairs for making a recommendation as to the date of commencement of a session of Parliament and its likely duration.

The recommendation, if agreed to by the Prime Minister, is submitted to the President for his approval of the date(s) of commencement of the session. After his approval, the date(s) of commencement and duration of the Session are conveyed to the Secretariats of Lok Sabha and Rajya Sabha for issuing of summons to Members of Parliament.

Sessions

Summoning

During the period from 1.4.98 to 31.12. 98, two sessions each of Lok Sabha and Rajya Sabha were held. The details of the sessions are given below:-

Session	Duration	Sittings	Days
	Twelfth Lok Sabha		
2nd	May 27 to August 6	38	72
3rd	November 30 to December 23	18	24
	Rajya Sabha		
184th	May 27 to August 4	35	70
185th	November 30 to December 23	18	24

Prorogation

After obtaining the approval of the Cabinet Committee on Parliamentary Affairs to prorogue the Houses, the Government's decision is conveyed to the two Secretariats of Parliament to enable them to issue the order of the President and to notify the same in the Gazette of India. The details of dates of adjournment sine-die and the prorogation of the two Houses by the President are as under:-

Session	Date(s) of: Adjournment sine-die	Date(s) of: Prorogation
	Twelfth Lok Sabha	
2nd	August 6, 98	August 10, 98
3rd	December 23, 98	December 31, 98
	Rajya Sabha	
184th	August 4, 98	August 10. 98
185th	December 23, 98	December 31, 98

Dates of Poll, Constitution, First Sitting Expiration of the Term and dissolution of Lok Sabha
(First to Twelfth Lok Sabha)

Lok Sabha	Last date of Poli	Date of the constitution	Date of the first Sitting	Date of expiration of term (Article 83(2) of the Constitution)	Date of Dissolution
1	2	3	4	5	6
First	21.02.52	02.04.52	13.05.52	12.05.57	04.04.57
Second	15.03.57	05.04.57	10.05.57	09.05.62	31.03.62
Third	25.02.62	02.04.62	16.04.62	15.04.67	03.03.67
Fourth	21.02.67	04.03.677	16.03.67	15.03.72	27.12.70
Fifth	10.03.71	15.03.71	19.03.71	18.03.77	18.01.77
Sixth	20.03.77	23.03.77	25.03.77	24.03.82	22.08.79
Seventh	06.01.80	10.01.80	21.01.80	20.01.85	31.12.84
Eighth	28.12.84	31.12.84	15.01.85	14.01.90	27.11.89
Ninth	26.11.89	02.12.89	18.12.89	17.12.94	13.03.91
1	2	3	4	5	6

(Contd. . .)

Tenth	15.06.91	20.06.91	09.07.91	08.07.96	10.05.96
Eleventh	07.05.96	15.05.96	22.05.96	21.05.2001	04.12.97
Twelfth	07.03.98	10.03.98	23.03.98	22.03.2003	

Number of Sittings of Parliament from 1952 to 1998

Year	Number of Sittings		Year	Number of Sittings	
Sabha	Lok Sabha	Rajya Sabha		Lok Sabha	Rajya
1	2	3	1	2	3
1952	103	60	1953	137	100
1954	137	103	1955	139	111
1956	151	113	1957	104	78
1958	125	91	1959	123	87
1960	121	87	1961	102	75
1962	116	91	1963	122	100
1964	122	97	1965	113	96
1966	119	109	1967	110	91
1968	120	103	1969	120	102
1970	119	107	1971	102	89
1972	111	99	1973	120	105
1974	119	109	1975	63	58
1976	98	84	1977	86	70
1978	115	97	1979	66	54
1980	96	90	1981	105	89
1982	92	82	1983	93	77
1	**2**	**3**	**1**	**2**	**3**
1984	77	63	1985	109	89
1986	98	86	1987	102	89
1988	102	89	1989	83	71

(Contd. . .)

1990	81	66	1991	90	82
1992	98	90	1993	89	79
1994	77	75	1995	78	77
1996	70	64	1997	65	68
1998	64	59			

3

President's Address and Ordinances

President's address

Article 87(l) enjoins upon the President to address both Houses of Parliament assembled together at the commencement of the first session after each General Election and also at the commencement of the first session of each calendar year. In accordance with clause (2) of Article 87, provisions has been made in the Rules of Procedure of the Lok Sabha and of the Rajya Sabha for discussion on the matters referred to in the President's Address.

The debate in both Houses takes place on a Motion of Thanks which is moved and seconded by members selected by the Minister of Parliamentary Affairs. The motion duly signed by such members are forwarded by the Ministry of Parliamentary Affairs to the Parliament Secretariat concerned. The scope of the discussion on the Address is very wide and members are free to speak on any subject, whether national or international.

Even matters not specifically mentioned in the Address are touched upon by members through tabling of amendments to the Motion of Thanks on the Address or through participation in the debate. The office of the President is not criticised for anything contained in the Address, as it is drafted by the Government.

The criticism, if any, has to be directed towards the Government. In 1998, the Address was delivered by the President on 25 March, 1998 at the commencement of first session after General Elections, 1998.

Provisions regarding ordinances

According to Article 123, if at any time, (except when both Houses of Parliament are in Session), the President is satisfied that circumstances exist which render it necessary for him to take immediate action, the President may promulgate an Ordinance as the circumstances appear to him to require. Such Ordinances shall have the same force and effect as an Act of Parliament but they should not contain any provision which Parliament would not under the Constitution be competent to enact.

The said Article further stipulates laying of Ordinances before both Houses of Parliament. Provision also exists for moving Statutory Resolutions seeking their disapproval. Under the Constitution, an Ordinance shall cease to operate at the expiration of six weeks from the reassembly of Parliament, or if before the expiration of that period.

Resolutions disapproving it are passed by both Houses, upon the passing of the second of those Resolutions. Where the Houses of Parliament are summoned on different dates, the period of six weeks shall be reckoned from the later of those dates. Provisions have been made in the Rules of Procedure of the two Houses for laying of statements explaining the circumstances which necessitated promulgation of Ordinances so that members might make use of the same while deliberating upon them.

The Ministry of Parliamentary Affairs ensures compliance of various provisions of the Constitution of India and the Rules of Procedure and Conduct of Business in the two Houses of Parliament by arranging laying of copies of the Ordinances, requesting the Ministries to lay explanatory statements and providing time for consideration of Resolutions seeking disapproval of the Ordinances alongwith consideration of Bills seeking to replace these Ordinances. All efforts are made to get action completed well within the period of six weeks as stipulated in the Constitution.

Ordinances

During the period from 1.4.98 to 31.12.1998, 16 Ordinances were promulgated by the President. Out of these sixteen Ordinances, eight Ordinances have been repromulgated. These Ordinances had to be re-promulgated because these could not be replaced by Acts of Parliament within stipulated period in terms of Article 123 (2) (a) of the Constitution.

Excluding one ordinance which was promulgated after prorogation of Winter Session, 1998, a copy each of the remaining fifteen Ordinances (English & Hindi versions) were duly laid by the Ministers of State in the Ministry of Parliamentary Affairs, on the Table of the Lok Sabha and Rajya Sabha as indicated in the following statement which also gives others details about their replacement, if any, by Acts of Parliament:-

Resolutions seeking disaproval of Ordinances were moved in respect of Ordinances mentioned at

Sl. No.	Title of the Ordinance & date of promullgation	Date of laying L.S.	Date of laying R.S.	Introduction of Bill replacing the Ordinance	Consideration and passing of the Bil L.S.	Consideration and passing of the Bil R.S	Date of ascent & Act No.
1	2	3	4	5	6	7	8.
1.	The Finance (Amendment) Ordinance, 1998 (No. 5 of 1998 (21.4.98)	27.5.98	28.5.98	29.5.98 (L.S.)	4.7.98	6.7.98	July 7, 98 / 16 of 1998
2.	The Lotteries (Regulation) Ordinance, 1198 (No. 6 of 1998) (23.4.98)	27.5.98	28.5.98	27.5.98 (L.S.)	4.7.98	6.7.98 7.7.98	July 7, 98 / 17 of 1998
3.	The Merchant Shipping (Amendment) Ordinance, 1998 (No. 7 of 1998) (233.4.98)	27.5.98	28.5.98	1.6.98 (R.S.)	10.6.98	3.6.98	June 6, 98 / 9 of 1998
4.	The Employees' Provident Funds and Miscellaneous Provisions	27.5.98	28.5.98	7.8.98 (R.S.)	9.6.97 10.6.98	1.6.98	June 22, 98 / 11 of 1998

(Contd. . .)

1	2	3	4	5	6	7	8
	(Amendment) Ordinance, 2222998 (No. 8 of 1998) (23.4.98)						
5.	The National Institute of Pharmaceutical Education and Research (Second) Ordinance, 1998 (No. 9 of 1998) (23.4.98)	27.5.98	28.5.98	28.5.98 (L.S.)	4.6.98	11.6.98	June 26, 98 / 13 of 1998
6.	The Payment of Gratuity (Amendment Ordinance, 1998 (No. 10 of 1998) (23.4.98)	27.5.98	28.5.98	24.7.97 (R.S.)	10.6.98	1.6.98 2.6.98	June 22, 98 / 11 of 1998
7.	The High Court and Supreme Court Judges (Conditions of Service) (Amendment) Ordinance, 1998	27.5.98	28.5.98	28.5.98 (L.S.)	4.7.98	6.7.98	July 7, 98 / 18 of 1998

(Contd. . .)

1	2	3	4	5	6	7	8
	(No. 11 of 1998) (24.4.98)						
8.	The Representation of the People (Amendment) Ordinance, 1998 (No. 12 of) 1 1998 (24.4.98)	27.5.98	28.5.98	1.6.98 (R.S.)	10.6.98	2.6.98	June 22, 98 / 12 of 1998
9.	The Essential Commodities (Amendment) Ordinance, 1998 (No. 13 of 1998 (25.4.98)	27.5.98	28.5.98	29.5.98 (L.S.)		Referred Committee Report 9.12.98	to Joint on 9.7.98 and presented on
10.	The Electricity Regulatory Commissions Ordinance, 1998 (No. 14 of 1998) (25.4.98)	27.5.98	28.5.98	3.6.98 (L.S.)	9.6.98	12.6.98	July 2, 98 / 14 of 1998
11.	The Central Vigilance Commission Ordinance, 1998 (No. 15 of 1998) (25.8.98)	2.12.98	30.11.98	7.12.98 (L.S.)	31.7.98		
12.	The Prasar Bharati	2.12.98	30.11.98	1.6.98 (L.S.)			

(Contd. . .)

1	2	3	4	5	6	7	8
	(Broadcasting Corporation of India) (Amendment) Ordinance, 1998 (No. 16 of 1998) (29.8.98)						
13.	The Oil-fields (Regulation and Development) (Amendment) Ordinance, 1998 (No. 17 of 1998) (3.9.98)	2.12.98	30.11.98	27.7.98 (L.S.)	2.12.98	8.12.98	Dec. 21, 98 / 20 of 1998
14.	The Central Vigilance Commission) (Amendment) Ordinance, 1998 (No. 18 of 1998) (27.10.98)	2.12.98	30.11.98	7.12.98 (L.S.)			
15.	The Companies (Amendment) Ordinance, 1998 (No. 19 of 1998) (31.10.98)	2.12.98	30.11.98	22.12.98 (L.S.)	22.12.98 (Discussed inconclusively)		

(Contd. . .)

1	2	3	4	5	6	7	8
16.	The Finance (No. 2) (Amendment) Ordinance, 1998 (No. 20 of 1998) (31.12.98)						

Ordinances Promulgated by the President from 1952 to 1998

Year	Number of Ordinances Promulgated	Year	Number of Ordinances Promulgated
1	2	3	4
1952	09	1953	07
1954	09	1955	07
1956	09	1957	06
1958	07	1959	03
1960	01	1961	03
1962	08	1963	–
1964	03	1965	07
1966	13	1967	09
1968	13	1969	10
1970	05	1971	23
1972	09	1973	04
1974	15	1975	29
1976	16	1977	16
1978	06	1979	10
1980	10	1981	12

(Contd. . .)

1	2	3	4
1982	01	1983	11
1984	15	1985	08
1986	08	1987	10
1988	07	1989	02
1990	10	1991	09
1992	21	1993	34
1994	14	1995	15
1996	32	1997	31
1998	20		

The position regarding Governments which were in power at the Centre during the years in which Ordinances were promulgated is as under:-

First Lok Sabha : April 2, 52 to April 4, 57: National Congress (Pandit Jawahar Lal Nehru)

Second Lok Sabha: April 5, 57 to March 31, 62: National Congress (Pandit Jawahar Lai Nehru)

Third Lok Sabha: April 2, 62 to March 3, 67: National Congress (Pandit Jawahar Lai Nehru from April 2, 62 to May 27, 1964, Shri Gulzari Lai Nanda from May 27, 1964 to June 9, 1964, Shri Lai Bahadur Shastri from June 9, 1964 to January 11, 1966 and Shri Gulzari Lai Nanda from January 11, 1966 to January 24, 1966 and Smt. Indira Gandhi from January 24, 1966 to March 3, 1967)

Fourth Lok Sabha:	March 4, 67 to December 27. 70: Congress (1) (Smt. Indira Gandhi)
Fifth Lok Sabha:	March 15, 71 to January 18, 77: Congress (1) (Smt. Indira Gandhi)
Sixth Lok Sabha:	March 23, 77 to August 22, 79: Congress (1)/Janata Party (Smt. Indira Gandhi 18.1.77 to 24.3.77) (Shri Morarji Desai from March 24, 77 to July 28, 79 and Shri Charan Singh from July 28, 79 to January 14, 80)
Seventh Lok Sabha:	January 10, 80 to December 31, 84: Congress (1) (Smt. Indira Gandhi from January 14, 80 to October 31, 84 and Shri Rajiv Gandhi from October 31, 84 to December 2. 89)
Eighth Lok Sabha:	December 31, 84 to November 27, 89: Congress (1) (Shri Rajiv Gandhi from October 31, 84 to December 2, 1989)
Ninth Lok Sabha:	December 2, 89 to March 13, 91: (Shri V.P. Singh from December 2, 89 to November 10, 90 and Shri Chandra Shekhar from November 10, 90 to June 21, 91)
Tenth Lok Sabha:	June 20, 91 to May 10, 96: Congress (1) Shri P.V. Narasimha Rao from June 21, 96 to May 16, 1996)
Eleventh Lok Sabha:	May 15, 96 to Dec. 4, 1997: Bharatiya Janata Party/United Front

	(i) (Shri Atal Bihari Vajpayee from May 16, 96 to June 1, 1996) : June 1, 96 to March 19, 1998 : United Front
	(ii) (Shri H.D. Deve Gowda from June 1, 96 to April 21, 1997 and Shri I.K. Gujral from April 21, 1997 to March 19, 1998)
Twelfth Lok Sabha:	March 10, 98 onwards: Bharatiya Janata Party (Shri Atal Bihari Vajpayee from March 19, 1998)

4

Government Business in Parliament

Government Business

In a Parliamentary democracy a major portion of work before the Parliament relates to Government Business. Planning of Government Business, therefore, assumes great significance. It becomes the responsibility of the Government to see that the time for this purpose is wisely and effectively utilised.

The Rules of Procedure and Conduct of Business in the Lok Sabha and the Rajya Sabha provide that on days allotted for transaction of Government Business, that Business shall have precedence and that Business shall be arranged in such order as the Presiding Officers of the two Houses may determine in consultation with the Leader of the respective Houses.

The function of planning and co-ordination of Government Business has been entrusted to the Ministry of Parliamentary Affairs. In the discharge of this function, the Ministry works under the directions of the Cabinet Committee on Parliamentary Affairs. Almost the entire time when the Parliament is at work, barring the Question Hour every day and two-and-half hours on Fridays, is at the disposal of Government for Government Business.

Government, however, readily agree to provide time for consideration of topics of urgent public importance as demanded by members from time to time and recommended by the Business Advisory Committees of the two Houses.

Planning of Government Business in the Parliament

Well before the commencement of Session of Parliament, all Ministries/Departments of the Government of India are requested to intimate their legislative and non-legislative proposals for consideration during the ensuing Session of Parliament. However, the programme for the Session is not finalised merely on the basis of replies received from the different Ministries/Departments.

The Ministry cross-checks the information with the Legislative Department of the Ministry of Law and Justice to ascertain the position in regard to drafting of the Bills. Thereafter, the Minister of Parliamentary Affairs takes a meeting of senior officers of Ministries Departments before the commencement of every session to impress upon them the necessity of giving priority to the finalisation of legislative proposals, and other items of Government Business.

Legislative proposals which are not ripe enough and are not likely to be ready intime are dropped. Two such meetings were held on 14.5.1998 and 10.11.1998 before the Budget and the Winter Sessions respectively. After having made a precise assessment of the Government Business, a calendar of Government Business is tentatively drawn up for each Session.

During the period from 1.4.1998 to 31.12.1998, two Tentative Lists of Government Business were prepared and made available to the Lok Sabha/Rajya Sabha Secretariats for circulation among Members through Parliamentary Bulletins. The Tentative List of Government Business enables members of Parliament to have a broad idea about the subjects that might come up in the Session and to make preparation for participation in debates thereon.

In order to give members advance information of the Government Business to be transacted by both Houses of Parliament, the Minister/Minister of State of Parliamentary Affairs makes statements in Lok Sabha and Rajya Sabha at the last sitting in each week regarding Government Business to be taken up in the succeeding week. 10 such statements in the Lok Sabha and 12 in the Rajya Sabha were made during the period under report.

The process of planning the programme of Government Business does not end by making a forecast once a week. The progress of Business is constantly and closely watched so that adjustments if needed, could be made at short notice. In actual practice, such adjustments are required to be made from day to day.

For this purpose, the Ministry supplied the order of Government Business for each sitting of the two Houses to the concerned Secretariat of Parliament for inclusion in the daily Order Paper. During the period under report, 61 lists of Government Business for the Lok Sabha and 67 for the Rajya Sabha were issued to the two Secretariats of Parliament in connection with transaction of Government Business.

Management of Government Business

Management of Government Business is important and requires a lot of skill and dexterity on the part of the Minister of Parliamentary Affairs. As the Chief Whip of the Party in power, he must at all times ensure the attendance of Members of the Party. He also keeps close and constant contact with the Presiding Officers, the Leaders as well as Chief Whips and Whips of various parties and Groups.

Resume of Government Business transacted

(i) Legislative

A total of 33 Bills were pending in Parliament at the

conclusion of First Session of Twelfth Lok Sabha and the 183rd Session of Rajya Sabha. 58 Bills (47 Bills in Lok Sabha and 11 Bills in Rajya Sabha) were introduced in two Houses during the period under report, making a total of 91 Bills. Out of these, 32 Bills were passed by both Houses during the period under report. Apart from this, one Bill namely, the Appropriation (No. 2) Bill, 1998 which was passed by Lok Sabha and transmitted to the Rajya Sabha was not considered by the Rajya Sabha.

However, interms of article 109(5) of the Constitution, this Bill being Money Bill was deemed to have been passed by both Houses after expiration of 14 days of its receipt in the Rajya Sabha. Therefore, the number of Bills passed by both Houses during the period under report is 33. This leaves a total of 58 Bills (22 Bills in Lok Sabha, 36 Bills in Rajya Sabha) pending in both Houses of Parliament' at the conclusion of Winter Session, 1998.

(ii) Financial

Rule 204 of the Lok Sabha Rules provides that the Annual Financial Statement interms of, article 112 of the Constitution popularly known as the "Budget" shall be presented to Parliament on such day as the President may direct. The Central Government Budget is presented in two parts—Railways and General. The former is presented about a week earlier than the General Budget which is normally presented on the last working day in the month of February.

The State Budgets in respect of States which are under President's rule, are also presented. The Budgets are presented to the Lok Sabha when the Minister-in-charge of Railways and Finance read their- Budget speeches. In Rajya Sabha, the Annual Financial Statement is laid, usually-after the completion of speech of the Minister in Lok Sabha.

One of the important decisions taken during the Budget Session, 1993 was to set up Department-related Parliamentary Standing Committees to scrutinise, inter-alia-the Demands for Grants of various Ministries/ Departments before these are discussed and voted in the House.

The other functions of the Standing Committees include examining Bills referred to them by the Chairman or Speaker, annual reports of Ministries and basic long terms policy documents presented to the Houses and referred to them by the Presiding Officers.

During the recess of Parliament in June-July, 1998, 17 Department related Parliamentary Standing Committees scrutinised inter-alia the Demands for Grants of various Ministries/Departments of the Government of India before these were discussed and voted in the House.

A statement giving the dates for consideration of the Railway Budget and General Budget during the period from 1.4.1998 to 31.12.1998 is appended.

(iii) Other official vusiness

The following other matters were considered on Official motions during the period from 1.4.1998 to 31 12 1998:-

Sl. No.	Subject	Lok Sabha Date(s)	Lok Sabha Time Taken Hrs–Mts	Rajya Sabha Date (s)	Rajya Sabha Time Taken Hrs–Mts

(Contd. . .)

1	2	3	4	5	6
1.	Discussion on the Final Report of the Jain Commission and Memorandum of Action Taken on the Report, laid on the Table of the House on 31.7.98	5.8.98 6.8.98	14.-28	3.8.98 4.8.98	8.25
2.	Discussion on the Thirtieth Report of the erstwhile Commissioner for Scheduled Castes and Scheduled Tribes for the years 1989-91.	8.12.98	2-35 (Inconclusive)	1.12.98 2.12.98 3.12.98 7.12.98	6.04
3.	Consideration and adoption of Resolution regarding draft Ministers' (Allowances, Medical Treatment and other Privileges) Amendment Rules, 19998 (Adopted)	22.12.98	–	23.12.98	–

5

Private Members' Business and Distribution of Parliamentary Time

Rules of Procedure and Conduct of Business in the Lok Sabha and the Rajya Sabha afford ample opportunities to members, who are not members of the Council of Ministers, to raise matters of urgent public importance and ventilate the grievances of the people at large through various devices like Calling Attention Notices, Short Duration Discussions, No-day- Yet-Named Motions, Censure Motions, Motions of No-Confidence in the Council of Ministers, Half-an-hour Discussions besides the Private Members' Bills and Resolutions which are taken up alternatively for two-and-a-half hours kept apart for Private Members' Business normally on Fridays. The following discussions were held during the period from 1.4.1998 to 31.12.1998—

Sl. No.	Subject and Member No.	Ministry concer-ned	Date (s) discus-sion	Time Taken Hrs-Mts
	Lok Sabha Discussion under rule 193			
1.	Discussion on the statement made by the Prime Minister in the House on 27 May 1998 on the recent nuclear tests in Pokhran (Shri Indrajit Gupta)	Defence	27.5.98 28.5.98 29.5.98	12-56

(Contd.)

2.	Discussion on incidents of suicide committed by farmers in various parts of the country due to non-payment of remunerative prices for their agricultural produce. (Shri Vilas Muttemwar)	Agriculture	1.6.98 2.6.98 3.6.98	10-04
3.	Discussion on rise in prices of essential commodities. (Shri Basudeb Acharia)	Food & Consumer Affairs	9.7.98	5-45
4.	Discussion on statement made by Minister of Industry on 8 June, 1998 regarding Maruti Udyog Ltd. (Shri S. Jaipal Reddy)	Industry	21.7.98	3-07
5.	Discussion on floods in various parts of the country. (Shri Mohan Singh)	Agricult-ure	22.7.98	4-35
6.	Discussion on increasing atrocities on women (Smt. Geeta Mukherjee)	Home Affairs	23.7.98 24.7.98 27.7.98 28.7.98	7-04
7.	Discussion on situation in North-Eastern region due to insurgency (Shri Bhubaneswar Kalita)	Home Affairs	29.7.98 31.7.98	5-45
8.	Discussion on the recent developments affecting India's Foreign Policy and on the statement made by the Prime Minister on his recent visit to Colombo in connection with SAARC Summit (Shri P.A. Sangma)	External Affairs	3.8.98 4.8.98	7-14
9.	Discussion on the statement made by the Home Minister of Home Affairs regarding Affairs departation of certain people by Maharashtra Government. (Shri Hannan Mollah)	Home Affairs	3.8.98 4.8.98	4-41
10.	Discussion on problems of Scheduled Castes and Scheduled Tribes. (Shri Ram Vilas Paswan)	Social	4.8.98	7-28

(Contd. . .)

1	2	3	4	5
11.	Discussion on rise in prices of essential commodities. (Shri Rajesh Pilot)	Food & Justice and Empowerment	3.12.98	10-39
12.	Discussion on atrocities committed on minorities in various parts of the country (Shri Arif Mohammad Khan)	Home Affairs	8.12.98 9.12.98	12-02
13.	Discussion on damage to crops due to natural calamities such as floods cyclones, etc. (Smt. Geeta Mukherjee)	Agriculture	21.12.98	1-29 (Inconclusive)
14.	Discussion on the statement made by the Prime Minister on 15 December, 1998 on bilateral talks with United States. (Shri Rupchand Pal)	External Affairs	22.12.98	2-21
	Rajya Sabha			
	Dlicussions under Rule 176			
1.	(i) Discussion on the statement made by the Prime Minister on 28 May, 1998 on recent nuclear tests in Pokhran (ii) Discussion on the statement made by Minister of Defence on 29 May, 1998 on Pakistan's Nuclear Test. (i) & (ii) discussed together on 29.5.1998	Defence	28.5.98 29.5.98	8-42
2.	Discussion on the alarming deterioration in the power and water supply in the country. (Shri S. B. Chavan)	Power & Rural Areas & Employment	11.6.98	3-24
3.	Discussion on the grave situation arising out of increase in subversive activities in North East region of the country. (Prof. Vijay Kumar Malhotra)	Home Affairs	15.7.98	4-20

(Contd. . .)

1	2	3	4	5
4.	Discussion on functioning of W.T.O. and participation of India in the International Trade negotiations (Shri Pranab Mukherjee)	Commerce	27.7.98	2-33
5.	Discussion on the dismissal of the Government of Goa. (Shri Kapil Sibal)	Home Affairs	30.7.98	2-07 (Inconclusive)
6.	Discussion on the current economic situation and its implications on various aspects of Indian economy including price rise and recession. (Shri Pranab Mukherjee)	Finance	7.12.98 8.12.98	5-35
7.	Discussion on Sugar Policy (Shri S. Ramachandra Reddy)	Food & Consumer Affairs	9.12.98 10.12.98	3-36
8.	Discussion on a statement on bilateral talks with the United States of America made by the Prime Minister. (Shri Pranab Mukherjee)	External Affairs	15.12.98	5-20
	Working of Ministreis Discussed in Rajya Sabha			
1.	External Affairs		9.7.98 10.7.98	6-24
2.	Human Resource Development		13.7.98 14.7.98 15.7.98	6-30
3.	Environment and Forests		21.7.98 22.7.98	6-15

Broad distribution of official time

The broad distribution of total official time taken by Legislative, Financial and Non-financial items (including debates arranged on Private Members' Motions during the time earmarked for transaction of official business) in both Houses of Parliament is as under:—

1	2	3	4	5
		Percentage		
Item	Lok Sabha Hrs. Mts.	Rajya Sabha Hrs. Mts.	Lok Sabha	Rajya Sabha
i) Legislative	28-48	32-32	16.19	15.37
ii) Financial	54-11	74-19	30.46	35.13
iii) Non-Financial	94-54	104—45	53.35	49.50

Time on interruptions/adjournments

During the period under report, Lok Sabha and Rajya Sabha were adjourned on various occasions due to various reasons. Time spent/lost on such interruptions/ adjournments etc. in Lok Sabha and Rajya Sabha during the period under report is indicated below:-

Session	Actual Total time Hrs Mts	Time Spent on interruptions adjournments due to discorderly scenes Hrs Mts	Percentage of time on interruptions etc. due to disorderly scenes
		Lok Sabha	
2nd	284-23	13-09	4.62
3rd	96-58	25-34	26.37
Total	381-21	38-43	10.15
		Rajya Sabha	
184th	233-56	9-26	4.03
185th	101-08	7-56	7.84
Total	335-04	17-22	5.18

Other non-official Business

During the period under report, 15 Calling Attention Notices (7 in Lok Sabha including one part discussed and 8 in Rajya Sabha) were discussed. The number of half-an-hour discussions were 4 in Lok Sabha and 5 in Rajya Sabha.

Government's stand on private member's bills and resolutions

One of the functions of the Cabinet Committee on Parliamentary Affairs is to determine Government's stand towards Private Member's Bills and Resolutions listed and put down for consideration in the two Houses of Parliament. During the period from 1.4.98 to 31.12.1998, the Ministries/Departments concerned were requested to send briefs on Government's stand on the Bills and Resolutions. Accordingly, briefs on 20 non-official Bills (12 in Lok Sabha and 8 in Rajya Sabha) and 14 non-official Resolutions (5 in Lok Sabha and 9 in Rajya Sabha) were placed before the Committee for determination of Government's stand thereon. The non-official Bills and Resolutions discussed during the period under report are listed below:

Private members' bills considered by the houses of parliament during the period from 1.4.98 to 31.12.98

Sl. No.	Name of the Bill and Member incharge	Date(s) of Discussion	Result
	Lok Sabha		
1.	The, Constitution (Amendment) Bill, 1998 (Insertion of new article 51B) by Shri Mohan Singh	12.6.98 10.7.98	Withdrawn
2.	The Constitution (Amendment) Bill, 1998 (Amendment of article 15 etc.) by Shri G.M. Banatwalla	10.7.98 24.7.98 4.12.98	Withdrawn
3.	The Land Acquisition (Amendment) Bill, 1998 (substitution of new section	4.12.98	Withdrawn

(Contd.)

	for section 16 etc.) by Shri Bhagwan Shanker Rawat		
4.	The Constitution (Amendment) Bill, 1998 (Insertion of new article 29A, etc.) by Shri Mohan Singh.	18.12.98	(Inconclusive
	RAajya Sabha		
1.	The Public Interest Litigation (Regulation) Bill, 1996 by Shri Suresh Pachouri	25.7.97 12.6.98	Withdrawn
2.	The Ragpickers and other Vagabond Street Children (Rehabilitation and Welfare) Bill, 1994 by Shri Ahmed Patel	12.6.98 10.7.98	Withdrawn
3.	The Prevention of Barbarous and Beastly Cruelty against Women Bill, 1995 by Miss Saroj Khaparde	10.7.98 24.7.98 4.12.98	Withdrawn
4.	The Hindu Marriage (Amendment) Bill, 1996 by Shri R. Margabandu	4.12.98	Withdrawn
5.	The Public Libraries Bill, 1998 by Shri Kartar Singh Duggal	4.12.98	Withdrawn
6.	The Constitution (Amendment) Bill, 1996 (to amend articles 124, 217, etc.) by Shri V.N. Gadgil	4.12.98	(Inconclusive)

Private members' resolutions considered by the Parliament during the period from 1.4.98 to 331.12.98

Sl. No.	Name of the Bill and Member incharge	Date(s) of Discussion	Result
	Lok Sabha		
1.	Resolution regarding National Housing Policy by Dr. Laxminarayan Pandey 17.7.98	2.6.98 5.6.98	Withdrawn
2.	Resolution regarding comprehensive policy to improve the functioning of Public Sector Undertakings by Dr. Asim Bala	17.7.98	(Inconclusive)
	Rajya Sabha		
1.	Resolution regarding review of the	5.6.98	Withdrawn

(Contd. . .)

	electoral system in the country by Shri Ramdas Agarwal.	3.7.98 17.7.98	
2.	Resolution regarding rise in prices of essential commodities by Shri Khagen Das	17.7.98	Negative

Private Members Bills Passed by Parliament from 1952 to 1998

Sl. No.	Short Title of the Bill	Act No. Date of Assent
	A. Bills introduced in the Lok Sabha	
1.	The Muslim Wakfs Bill, 1952 by Shri Syed Mohammed Ahmed Kasmi	29 of 1954 21.05.1954
2.	The Indian Registration (Amendment) Bill, 1955 by Shri S.C. Samanta.	17 of 1956 06.04.1956
3.	The Parliamentary Proceedings (Protection of Publication) Bill, 1956 by Shri Feroze Gandhi	24 of 1956 26.05.1956
4.	The Code of Criminal Procedure (Amendment) Bill, 19533 by Shri Raghunath Singh	39 of 1956 01.09.1956
5.	The Women's and Children's Institutions (Licensing) Bill, 1954 by Rajmata Kamlendu Mati Shah	105 of 1956 30.12.1956
6.	The Code of Criminal Procedure (Amendment) Bill, 1957 by Smt. Subhadra Joshi	56 of 1960 26.12.1960
7.	The Salaries and Allowances of Members of Parliament (Amendment) Bill, 1964 by Shri Raghunath Singh.	26 of 1964 29.09.1964
8.	The Hindu Marriage (Amendment) Bill, 1963 by Shri Diwan Chand Sharma.	44 of 1964 20.12.1964
9.	The Supreme Court (Enlargement of Criminal Appellate Jurisdiction) Bill, 1968 by Shri Anand Narain Mullah.	28 of 1970 09.08.1970
	B. Bills Introduced in the Rajya Sabha	
10.	The Ancient And Historical Monuments and	70 of 1956

(Contd.)

	Archeological Sites and Remains (Declaration of National Importance) Bill, 1954 by Dr. Raghubir Singh.	15.12.1956
11.	The Hindu Marriage (Amendment) Bill, 1956 by Dr. (Smt.) Seeta Parmanand.	73 of 1956 20.12.1956
12.	The Orphanages and Other Charitable Homes (Supervision and Control) Bill, 1960 by Shri Kailash Bihari Lal.	10 of 1960 09.04.1960
13.	The Marine Insurance Bill, 1959 by Shri M.P. Bhargava.	11 of 1963 18.04.1963
14.	The Indian Penal Code (Amendment) Bill, 1963 by Shri Diwan Chaman Lall.	36 of 1969 07.09.1969

6

Monitoring of Implementation of Assurances

While replying to questions or supplementaries thereon or during discussion on Bills, Resolutions, Motions in Parliament, at times, Ministers give certain assurances, such as, that they will consider the matter, take action, furnish the required information etc. The Government are obliged to fulfil these assurances and present a Report. Ministry of Parliamentary Affairs is the coordinating agency to ensure that the Ministry fulfil their assurances in time.

General procedure

The Ministry extracts from the daily proceedings of both Houses, assurances given by Ministers and forward the same to the Ministries/Departments concerned for taking necessary action thereon. There is a set of expressions for each House which constitute assurance to be fulfilled by the Government. These expressions are illustrative and not exhaustive. While treating statement of Minister as an assurance due consideration is given to the context in which it has been made and whether it is capable of being fulfilled within a reasonable time–frame.

All assurances given to the Parliament are required to be fulfilled within a period of three months. Where delay is anticipated by the Ministry on account of some genuine difficulties in fulfilling an assurance, the Committee on Government Assurances Lok Sabha/Rajya Sabha are approached for grant of extension of time. In case the Ministry/Department do not find it feasible to fulfil an assurance for any valid reason, on the request of the Ministry, the Committee on Government Assurances Lok Sabha/Rajya Sabha are approached to consider their request for dropping the assurance.

The Reports are laid on the Table of the Lok Sabha and the Rajya Sabha by the Minister/Minister of State of Parliamentary Affairs. Copies of the Reports laid are supplied to the Members concerned and are also kept in the Parliament Library. The details of Assurances/ extracted/fulfilled during the years 1985 to 1998 and the balance which remain to be implemented are as under:–

Lok Sabha

Year	Number of Assurances recorded	During the Year under	Number of Assurances fulfilled/dropped			Balance	Percentage of Implementation
	Total	report	Total	Fulfilled	Dropped		
1985	1122	–	1121		–	1	99.91%
1986	1688	–	1686	–	–	2	99.88%
1987	2139	–	2134	5	–	5	99,76%
1988	2308	–	2300	4	–	8	99.65%
1989	1794	–	1777	4	2	17	99.05%
1990	2408		2378	5	1	30	98.75%
1991	1717	5	1679	10	–	38	97.78%
1992	2229	5	2174	23	–	55	97.53%
1993	1798	6	1720	23	–	78	95.71%

(Contd. . .)

1994	1464	8	1371	30	–	93	93.64%
1995	1522	34	1379	69*	–	143	90.60%
1996	1696	51	1403	186*	13	293	82.73%
1997	1382	45	1046	381	8	336	75.68%
1998	1175	1175	231	231	–	944	19.65%
	24442	1329	22399	971	24	2043	91.64%

Rajya Sabha

Year	Number of Assurances recorded	During the Year under	Number of Assurances fulfilled/dropped			Balance	Percentage of Implementation
	Total	report	Total	Fulfilled	Dropped		
1985	1315	–	1314	–	–	1	99.22%
1986	1295	–	1295	–	–	–	100.00%
1987	1810	–	1801	9	1	9	99.50%
1988	1703	–	1698	4	1	5	99.70%
1989	1376	–	1357	5	–	19	98.61%
1990	1641	–	1606	4	–	35	97.86%
1991	1388	–	1363	4	1	25	98.19%
1992	2086	–	2061	20	3	25	98.80%
1993	1623	–	1587	18	1	36	97.78%
1994	1439	–	1357	29	–	82	94.30%
1995	1182	–	1079	43	3	103	91.28%
1996	738	–	613	85	2	125	83.06%
1997	773	5	558	217	3	215	72.18%
1998	753	753	126	126	–	627	16.73%
	19122	758	17815	564	15	1307	93.16%

In addition to the above, 47 part Implementation Reports relating to the Lok Sabha and 17 part Implementation Reports relating to Rajya Sabha were also laid, during the period under report.

Action to clear pending assurancess

The Ministry of Parliamentary Affairs has been vigorously pursuing with all the Ministries/ Departments for ensuring early implementation of Assurances given to Parliament. Periodic reviews are undertaken of all pending assurances and the Ministries/Departments are reminded to expedite implementation of the same. On 25.06.1998, the Minister of State for Railways, Parliamentary Affairs and Planning & Programme Implementation wrote to his Cabinet colleagues/Ministers of State, emphasizing the importance and need to speed up the implementation of assurances and for bringing about qualitative improvement in the replies given. The response from the Ministries/Departments shows that they are taking keen interest in the fulfilment of assurances.

The Ministry also undertook a scrutiny of all pending assurances with a view to bring out such assurances as have remained pending due to differences in the policy perceptions of the Governments/have lost relevance over the time/involve genuine difficulties in implementation or collection of voluminous information from various sources which is not forthcoming/which relate to controversial matters/cannot be dealt within the limited scope of question/assurance/within a prescribed time frame, for taking up with the Committee on Government Assurances of the Lok Sabha/Rajya Sabha for dropping. The matter is further, being examined in consultation with the Ministries concerned at the Secretary level.

Report of the committee on government assurances

The Committee on Government Assurances, Lok Sabha presented three reports, namely; I Report to the House on 08.12.1998 and II & III Reports on 17.12.1998 and Committee on Government Assurances Rajya Sabha presented its 44th & 45th Reports on 7th July, 1998 and 46th Reports on 21.12.1998 respectively.

7

Matters Raised Under Rule 377 in the Lok Sabha and Rajya Sabha

Matters raised under Rule 377 (Lok Sabha)

Under Rule 377 of the Rules of Procedure and Conduct of Business in the Lok Sabha, Members are allowed to raise matters which are not points of order or which cannot be raised under any other Rule. Members are required to give notice for raising a matter under this Rule in a standard form enclosing the text of the statement not exceeding 250 words.

Notice should be given by 10 hours of the day on which a matter is sought to be raised by the Member. Notices received after 10 hours on a day are deemed to have been given for the next sitting of the House. Notices tabled by Members between 10 hours and 10.30 hours on the last working day of the week are ballotted to determine inter–se–priority of Members for raising matters in the following week. The matters can be raised only with the permission of the Speaker. Under the Rule, a Member can raise only one 'matter' during a week.

At the meeting of Hon'ble Speaker with Leaders of Parties and Groups held on 18th November, 1997, it has been decided that as the matters which are meant for being raised under Rule 377 are increasingly being raised during Zero Hour, the number of matters presently being raised under Rule 377 be increased from 8 to 24 per day to be allocated on the basis of strength of parties/groups in Lok Sabha.

Members might read the brief subject of the text of their notices, given by the Secretariat, and the text of the matter might be treated as laid on the Table. The item might be taken up at 5.30 p.m. This procedure was followed during first Session of XII Lok Sabha. However, at the meeting of Business Advisory Committee held during Budget Session on 29.5.98, it was decided that the item relating to matters under rule 377 will be taken up after Question Hour and other formal items listed in the agenda paper as per direction 2 of the Directions by the Speaker regarding relative precedence of different classes of business.

It had also been decided that 12 Members instead of 24 will be allowed to raise the matters under rule 377 per day to be allocated on the basis of strength of Parties/Groups in Lok Sabha and that the Members will also be permitted to read the text of the matter. This procedure for raising matters under Rule 377 in Lok Sabha is therefore in vogue since Budget Session 1998 of Parliament.

Special mentions made in Rajya Sabha

In the Rajya Sabha there is no Rule corresponding to Rule 377 of the Lok Sabha Rules enabling members to raise such matters. However, a convention has been established whereby Members may raise matters of urgent public importance by way of "Special Mentions" with the permission of the Chairman. Ordinarily not more that one "Special Mention" by a Member is permitted on one subject. In case, notices are received from more than one Member on the same subject as the same time and for the same day, it is for the Chairman in his discretion to decide which Member has to be permitted to made the Special Mention. A Member should not take more than three minutes to make a "Special Mention".

A Member who desires to make a Special Mention has to give a notice in a standard form by 5.00 p.m. of the day preceeding the day on which he proposes to mention the matter in the House. The text of the matter proposed to be raised by Members is not required to be given alongwith the Notice.

Normally Ministers do not make statements or react to these matters raised on the floor of the two Houses. However, if a Minister so desires, he may make a statement on the subject with the permission of the Presiding Officer. The main advantage of this device is to bring to the notice of the House and the Government, the matters and happenings of urgent public importance which take place in or outside the country and have a bearing on our national interests and about which Members are agitated and for which Members may not get an early opportunity to raise these under any other Rule of the House.

Follow–up action

The extracts of the proceedings relating to these matters raised in two Houses are sent to the Ministries concerned by the Parliament Secretariat normally on the day following the day on which the matters are raised. The Ministry of Parliamentary Affairs also send weekly statements containing the gists of the matters raised in the two Houses to the Ministries concerned to enable them to cross–check the matter (s) raise in respect of their Ministry with reference to the extracts received by them from two Secretariats with a view to ensuring that no item is lost sight of. The Ministries are expected to take action on each of the points raised by Members and communicate the results to the Members concerned under intimation to the concerned Parliament Secretariat and the Ministry of Parliamentary Affairs within a period of one month from the date on which the matter is raised in the House. In order to ensure expeditious disposal of pending matters, the Ministry of Parliamentary Affairs send reminders to the Ministries from time to time at the level of Secretary and if necessary, at the Minister's level,

During the period under report, the Secretary, Ministry of Parliamentary Affairs also held meetings with his counterparts and other senior officers in various Ministries/Departments to review pendency of these matters in those Ministries. These meetings had tremendous effect on the dispose of pending matters concerning various Ministries/Departments. The meetings resulted in disposal of as many as 54% pending matters in the Lok Sabha and 40% pending matters in the Rajya Sabha, which were pending in the two Houses at the time of holding of these meetings.

During the period from 1.4.98 to 31.12.98, 557 matters were raised in Lok Sabha and 191 matters were raised in Rajya Sabha. Replies in respect of 351 Lok Sabha matters have been sent to the members concerned leaving a pendency of 206 matters as on 31.12.98. As regards the Rajya Sabha replies in respect of 112 Special Mentions have been sent to the Members concerned and the remaining 79 matters were still pending as on 31.12.98.

Action on matters raised after the question hour

After the Question flour every day, Members in both Houses raise, with the permission of the Presiding Officer, matters of urgent public importance. Sometimes, matters are also raised by Members without prior permission. It is not mandatory on the part of the Ministers to reply to such points immediately when they are raised in the House or subsequently through formal communications although sometimes, Ministers do react in the House to the points raised by the Members. The Minister of Parliamentary Affairs/Minister of State of Parliamentary Affairs, sometimes, intervene on such occasions and assure the House that the points raised by them would be brought to the notice of the Ministers concerned for necessary action. The Presiding Officers also give directions/make observations on various issues raised in the two Houses during Zero Hour.

Whenever Presiding officers give directions or the Minister/Ministers of State for Parliamentary Affairs intervene in the debate during Zero Hour and assure the House that the issue raised by the Members or the directions/observations thereon by the Presiding Officer would be brought to the notice of the Minister (s) concerned, the Ministry of Parliamentary Affairs forward the relevant extracts from the proceedings of the House to the Minister (s) concerned under the signature of the Minister or Minister of State for Parliamentary Affairs preferably on the same day, for necessary action.

8

Consultative Committee

The present Consultative Committees of Members of Parliament in their broad features, owe their origin to the suggestions set out by the late Prime Minister Shri Jawahar Lal Nehru in 1954 in a note circulated to the Members of Cabinet. Shri Nehru wanted some kind of Standing Advisory Consultative Committees of Parliament to provide opportunity to Members to have some glimpase into the working of the Government which would also have the effect of reducing the number of questions asked by Members.

Accordingly, Informal Consultative Committees were constituted for the various Ministries/Departments of the Government of India. In 1969, discussions were held with leaders of Opposition Parties/Groups in Parliament and detailed guidelines were drawn up for constitution and functioning of these Committees. It was also then decided that these Committees would be known as "Consultative Committees" retaining, however, the informal nature of deliberations in these Committees. These Committees have, since 'then, been functioning under these guidelines.

The main features of these Committee are as under:

(i) The membership of these Committees is voluntary and is left to the choice of the Members and the Leaders of their Parties.

(ii) The main objective of these Committees is informal consultation between the Government and the Members of Parliament on the policies and programmes of the Government and the manner of implementation thereof.

(iii) The Committees are chaired by the Minister incharge of the Ministries to which the Committees relate.

(iv) The maximum membership of a Committee is 40. The Committees are normally constituted if there are 10 or more Members who have chosen to be nominated on the Committee.

(v) Members can be nominated as Permanent Special Invites on a Consultative Committee if they have special interest in the subjects of a particular Ministry/Department. The maximum number of Permanent Special Invites on, a Consultative Committee can be 4 Members (hitherto for only two Permanent Special Invites could be nominated on a Consultative Committee).

(vi) Meetings of these Committees are held both during Session periods and Inter-session periods.

(vii) Agenda items are either called from Members or decided by the Ministry themselves in consultation with the Members of the Committee,

(viii) Members, who are not Members of a Committee, may be invited to the meetings of the Committee as special invites if they have given notice of any subject for inclusion in the agenda and the same has been included in the agenda, or if they "press their desire to participate in the discussion of any meeting of such Committee and the same has been approved by the Minister of Parliamentary Affairs.

(ix) No decision are taken by these Committees. However, where there is unanimity of view in the Committee,

Government will normally accept the few subject to certain conditions laid down in the guidelines.

(x) Senior Officers of the Ministries are present at the meeting to assist the Ministers and to furnish any clarifications required.

(xi) In keeping with the informal nature of discussion at the meeting, the Guidelines make it incumbent on the Members and also on the Government not to mention on the floor of either House about any thing that happens in these Committees.

Consultative committees

After General Election to the Twelfth Lok Sabha, 29 Consultative Committees for the various Ministries/ Departments were constituted in June./August, 1998.

Sub-committes/study groups of consultative committees

The Consultative Committee have been setting up Sub-Committes/Study Groups for the purpose of going into any particular aspect of the working of the concerned Ministry and submitting reports for consideration of the Committee. During the period under report, no Sub-Committee of the Consultative Committee was constituted.

Informal consultative committees of railway zones

Informal Consultative Committees of Members of Parliament are constituted for the Railway Zones. There are nine such Committees functioning at present. An the Members of Parliament belonging to the areas of particular Railway Zone are nominated on the Informal Consultative Committee of that Railway Zone. The discussion at these meetings are purely informal, Members are at liberty to raise any point relating to the working of Railway in their zones.

The meetings of these Committees are held only during the session periods. No TA/DA is required to be paid for attending Informal Consultative Committee meeting. During the period under report, meetings of the following Informal Consultative Committees were held:

Name of Informal Consultative Committee	Date of Meeting
(i) Central Railway Zone	8.12.98
(ii) Eastern Railway Zone	15.12.98
(iii) Northern Railway Zone	22.12.98

Meetings of consultative committees outside Delhi

As per instructions, one meeting of a Consultative Committee can be held outside Delhi in a year during an inter-session period in India. During the period under report, meetings of the Consultative Committees of the following Ministries were held outside Delhi:

Sl. No.	Name of Ministry	Date of meeting/place
1.	Coal	4.9.98 Puri (Orissa)
2.	Civil Aviation	9.9.98 Mumbai
3.	Defence	25.9.98 Avadi, Chennai
4.	Health &. Family Welfare	14.10.98 & 15.10.98 Thiruvananthapuram
5.	Surface Transport	23.10.98 Mumbai
6.	Rural Areas & Employment puram	26.10.98 Thiruvanantha-
7.	Power	3.11.98 Goa
8.	Textiles	12.11.98 Surat (Gujarat)

Other committees, boards, councils, etc

Committees are appointed to deal with specified items of business requiring expert or detailed consideration. There are two types of Committees. Official Committees i.e. those appointed by Government and Parliamentary Committees i.e. those appointed by Lok Sabha and Rajya Sabha or by the Presiding Officers of the two Houses of Parliament,

Government Committees are composed of Experts Officials and Non-officials, including, sometimes Members of Parliament.

Nomination of members of Parliament on Committees, Councils, Boards, Commissions etc. set- up by the Government

Members of Parliament are nominated by the Minister of Parliamentary Affairs on the various Committees, Councils, Boards, Commissions etc. set up by the Government of India in the various Ministries.

Nomination of members of Parliament on Hindi Salahkar Samitis

Members of Parliament are associated with the Hindi Salahkar Samitis constituted by each Ministry/Department to advise them on matters relating to the progressive use of Hindi in official work and allied issues falling within the framework of Official Language Policy laid down by the Government of India. The term of these Salahkar Samitis is normally three years. Four Members of Parliament (two from Lok Sabha and two from Rajya Sabha) are nominated on each of these Samitis by the Minister of Parliamentary Affairs.

Withdrawal of nomination of members of Parliament from Zonal Railway Users Consultative Committees (ZRUCCs) and the Divisional Railway Users Consultative Committees (DRUCCs)

As per the then instructions, 3 MPs (2 from Lok Sabha and 1 from Rajya Sabha) were nominated on each of the 9 ZRUCCs pertaining to different Railway Zones and 2 MPs (1 from Lok Sabha 1 from Rajya Sabha) were nominated on each of the 58 DRUCCs pertaining to different Railway Divisions. But according to the revised instructions of the Ministry of Railways, all the Members of Parliament hailing from the territorial jurisdiction of a railway zone have to be nominated on the ZRUCC of that zone.

As regards DRUCCs, one nominee of Member of Parliament has to be nominated on each of the DRUCCs falling in the constituency of that Member of Parliament. Since all the Members coming from a particular zone have to be nominated on that ZRUCC and there was no question of selection of Members, the Ministry of Railways was allowed to go ahead with the nomination of MPs on ZRUCCs and the nomination of MPs made on different DRUCCs was withdrawn.

Recommendations of general application by Parliamentary Committees

Ministry of Parliamentary Affairs is concerned with processing of action by Ministries on the recommendations of general application made by Parliamentary Committees. Action on the recommendation of general nature contained in the following reports was initiated by the Ministry:-

(i) Hundred-sixth, Hundred-seventh, Hundred-eighth, Hundred-ninth and Hundred-tenth Reports of the Committee on Petitions, Rajya Sabha.

(ii) First, Second and Third Reports of the Committee on Papers Laid on the Table of the Lok Sabha (12th Lok Sabha)

(iii) Sixty-second, Sixth-third, Sixty-fourth, Sixth-fifth, Sixty-sixth, Sixty-seventh and Sixty-eighth Reports of the Committee on Papers Laid on the Table of the Rajya Sabha.

(iv) First and Second Reports of Committee on Subordinate Legislation (12th Lok Sabha.)

9

Exchange of Government Delegations of Parliamentarians

In the continuously and rapidly changing international scenario, the need to project and propogate our national policies, programmes and problems in the proper perspective among various countries as well as understanding their view-point was being felt for a long time. The parliamentarians of a country play a significant role in determining the policy of the country and strengthening of relations with other countries. More particularly, it is indeed useful and necessary for a democratic and developing country like India, to select some Members of Parliament and distinguished personalities and utilize their service in projecting our policies, programmes, problems and achievements in different fields with their counterparts and other opinion makers in other countries and secure their confidence in favour of India. Undoubtedly, to achieve the aforesaid objectives, the exchange of Government sponsored delegations of Members of Parliament proved to be effective. Therefore, it was decided that three to four delegations consisting of Members of Parliament, under the leadership of Minister of Parliamentary Affairs/ Ministers of State for Parliamentary Affairs be sent abroad and also to invite three to four such delegations from other countries through the Ministry of Parliamentary Affairs yearly on a regular basis.

An amount of Rs. 1.10 crore in the budget of this Ministry for the year 1998-99 has beer provided for this purpose.

Visit of Government Sponsored delegation of MPs to foreign countries

Pursuant to the decision to exchange Government delegation consisting of Members of Parliament, the Ministry of Parliamentary Affairs arranged a visit of a Delegation of 9 Members Parliament under leadership of Shri Madan Lal Khurana, Hon'ble Minister of Parliamentary Affairs and Tourism to Singapore, Indonesia, Malaysia and Thailand during 20-29 September, 1998.

The objective of the visit was to effectively project our policies, achievements and programmes in those countries and thereby create an understanding among them about the Indian polity and the Government. The visit was also intended to meet the Presiding Officers and other parliamentarians those countries and to exchange views about our Parliamentary procedures and practices etc. The Members of the Delegation were chosen in consultation with their leaders/Chief Whips. The Delegation consisted of the following:

1. Shri Madan Lal Khurana, Minister of Parliamentary Affairs & Tourism — Leader

Lok Sabha

2. Capt. Jagatvir Singh Drona — BJP (UP)
3. Shri Ram Narain Meena — INC (Rajasthan)
4. Shri Rupchand Pal — CPI(M) (West Bengal)
5. Shri Mohan Singh — Samajwadi Party (UP)
6. Shri Kanchi Paneerselvarn — AIADMK (Tamil Nadu)
7. Shri Surender Prasad Yadav (Jhanjharpur) — R.J.D. (Bihar)

Rajya Sabha

8. Smt. Chandresh Kumari INC (Himachal Pradesh)

9. Shri Nilotpal Basu CPI (M) (West Bengal)

10. Shri K.M. Saifulla TDP (Andhra Pradesh)

Officers

11. Shri S.A.T. Rizvi, Secretary, Ministry of Parliamentary Affairs

12. Shri D.R. Tiwari, Joint Secretary, Ministry of Parliamentary Affairs

13. Shri S.C. Poddar, Private Secretary to Minister of Parliamentary Affairs & Tourism

It was decided that during the course of the visit the Members of Delegation would have meetings with Executive/Administrative Heads of the following subjects, beside meeting important legislative functionaries in these countries:

1. Tourism;
2. Education;
3. Legal System with emphasis on relationship between Judiciary and Legislatures;
4. Housing Problem;
5. Transport System; and
6. Family Planning and Population.

The delegation, during its stay at Singapore, met H.E. Mr. Tan Soo Khoon, Speaker of Parliament and Mr. Yatiman Yusof, Leader of Singapore West-Asia and Africa Parliamentary Group, besides various Buddhist Organisations. In Indonesia the delegation met H.E. Mr. Ida Bagus Oka, Minister for Population and Chairman of the National Planning Board, Indonesia, H.E. Mr. Juwono Sudarsono, Minister of Education and Culture, Indonesia,

H.E. Mr. Marzuki Usman, Minister of Tourism, Arts and Culture and H.E. Mr. Hary Sabarno, Deputy Speaker of MPR/DPR.

In Malaysia the delegation met Dato' Sabaruddin Chik, Malaysian Minister for Culture, Art and Tourism, Tan Sri Mohamed Bin Yacob, President of Senate, Malaysia and had a meeting with Buddhist Monks.

On the last leg of the visit in Thailand the delegation met His Holiness Maha Sangh Raja, the Supreme Patriarch of Thailand, Dr. Arthit Ourairat, Chairman, Foreign Relations Committee, Mr. Paijit Sreewaraken, Chairman, Parliamentary Affairs Committee, Thailand, Mr. Seree Wangpaichir, Governor, Tourism Authority of Thailand and H.E. Mr. Wanmuhamad Nor Matta, President of National Assembly, Thailand.

Nomination of members of parliament on the delegations going abroad

Minister of Parliamentary Affairs nominates or approves the names of Members of Parliament for the delegation being sent abroad by various Ministries. During the year, 1998 the names of the following Members of Parliament in the delegation noted against each of them were recommended/ nominated:-

1. Smt. Rita Verma, MP(LS)	USA-International
2. Smt. Ila Panda, MP (RS)	Conference on Girls Education (Ministry of HRD)
3. Prof. Vijay Kumar Malhotra, MP (RS)	
4. Shri Prem Singh Chandumajra, MP (LS)	Malaysia Official Delegation to
5. Shri Chetan Chauhan, MP (LS)	Commonwealth Games, 1998

6.	Shri Ajit Panja, MP (LS)	(Ministry of HRD)
7.	Shri Virender Singh, MP (LS) rians Conference on	China-6th General Assembly of the Asia-Pacific Parliamenta- Environment & Development
8.	Shri B.P. Singhal, MP (RS)	· Thailand-Official Delegation to 13th Asian Games, 1998
9.	Shri Akhilesh Dass, MP (RS)	(Ministry of HRD)

Meetings with Parliamentary delegations

During the period from 1.4.1998 to 31.12-1998, Nine Parliamentary Delegations, during their visit to India from various countries, called on Minister of Parliamentary Affairs and Tourism for exchange of views on matters of mutual interest. The details of such delegations are given below:

1.	11 April, 1998	A 5 Member DPR Korean Delegation led by H.E. Mr. Hyong Sop, Speaker of the Supreme- People's Assembly of DPR Korea.
2.	10 July, 1998	A 3 Member Venezuelan delegation led by H.E. Deputy Julio Castillo, First Vice President, Chairman of Deputies.
3.	28 August, 1998	A 3 Member Delegation led by H.E. Mr. Cyril E. Ndebele, Speaker, Parliament of Zimbabwe.
4.	15 September, 1998	A 16 Member Delegation led by H.E. Mr. Lawrent Fabius, President (Speaker) of the French National Assembly and former P.M. of France.
5.	16 September, 1998	A 7 Member Russian Delegation led by H.E. Mr. Vladimir Petrovich Lukin, Chairman, State Duma Committee on International Affairs, Russia.

6.	9 October, 1998	A 3 Member Sudanese Delegation led by Dr. Salah Eldin Hirgahani M.A. Gaili, Chairman of the Delegation and Deputy Chairman, Federal Relations Committee, Sudan.
7.	16 November, 1998	A 13 Member Delegation led by H.E. Mo. Mikko Pesala, Deputy Speaker of the Finnish Parliament
8.	24 November, 1998	A 9 Member Delegation led by H.E. Mr. Kozo Watanabe, Vice Speaker of the House of Representatives of Japanese Parliament.
9.	15 December, 1998	A 10 Member Delegation led by H.E. Mr. Antonio De Almeida Santos, President of the Portuguese Parliament.

Visit of members of Parliament to foreign countries

69 Members of Parliament (43 Members of Lok Sabha and 26 Members of Rajya Sabha) informed this Ministry about their private/study visits of foreign countries; Necessary assistance, when asked, was extended to them through the Ministry of External Affairs and our Missions in foreign countries.

Permission under foreign contribution (regulation) Act, 1976

Under the Foreign Contribution (Regulation) Act, 1976, it is incumbent on Members of Parliament, among others, going abroad, to obtain prior permission of the Ministry of Home Affairs where such visits involve acceptance of, 'foreign hospitality' from a foreign Government of organisation. Members are informed about the procedure to be followed in this respect from time to time by this Ministry. All necessary assistance sought for by Members in this regards is also provided.

10

Youth Parliament Scheme

Youth parliament competition in the schools

With a view to develop democratic ethos in younger generation, the Youth Parliament Competition was introduced for the first time in the country in the Higher Secondary Schools of the National Capital Territory of Delhi in 1966-67 by this Ministry in collaboration with the Directorate of Education, Government of Delhi. Since then, these competitions have been held every year in the Higher/Senior Secondary Schools in Delhi. A Prize Distribution Function is organised by the Ministry at the conclusion of the competition each year at which Prize Winning Schools and individual students and teachers-in-charge are given certificates and medals/trophies. The schools standing first is given the Pandit Motilal Nehru Running Parliamentary Shield instituted by this Ministry. Details of the number of participating schools, name of the school standing first etc. since 1966 are indicated below:-

Sl. No.	Year	Competition	No of participating Schools	Name of the School Standing first
1.	1966-67	First	16	Govt. Boy's Model Hr. Sec. School, Ludlow Castle, Delhi.
2.	1967-68	Second	25	S.B. Mill, Hr. Sec. School, Najafgarh Road, Delhi.

3.	1968-69	Third	43	Lady Irwin Hr. Sec. School, Canning Road, New Delhi.
4.	1969-70	Fourth	42	Lady Irwin Hr. Sec. School, Canning Road, New Delhi.
5.	1970-71	Fifth	41	Lady Irwin Hr. Sec. School, Canning Road, New Delhi.
6.	1971-72	Sixth	50	Govt. Girls' Hr. Sec. School, Sarojini Nagar, New Delhi.
7.	1972-73	Seventh	43	Andhra Education Society Hr.Sec. School, Rouse Avenue, New Delhi.
8.	1973-74	Eighth	50	Lady Irwin Hr. Sec. School, Canning Road, New Delhi.
9.	1974-75	Ninth	49	DTEA Hr. Sec. School, Laxmibai Nagar, New Delhi.
10.	1975-76	Tenth	52	DTEA Hr. Sec. School, Laxmibai Nagar, New Delhi.
11.	1976-77	Eleventh	52	Nav Hind Girls' Hr. Sec. School, Rohtak Road, New **Delhi.**
12.	1977-78	Twelfth	48	Govt. Girl's Sr. Sec. School No. I Rajouri Garden, New Delhi.
13.	1978-79	Thirte-enth	52 (inclu-ding 8 KV)	DTEA Hr. Sec. School, Pusa Road, Karol Bagh, New Delhi.
14.	1979-90	Fourte-enth	52 (inclu--ding KV)	Govt. Girls Sr. Sec. School, Adarsh Nagar, New Delhi.
15.	1980-81	Fifte-enth	52 (inclu-ding KV)	K.V. No. 1, Sector-IV, Faridabad, Haryana.
16.	1981-82	Sixteenth	52	Shri S.D. Girls Sr. Sec. School, East Patel Nagar, New Delhi.

(Contd. . .)

17.	1982-83	Seventeenth	62	K.V. Andrews Ganj, New Delhi.
18.	1983-94	Eighteenth	38	Govt. Girls Sr. Sec. School, Ramesh Nagar, New Delhi.
19.	1984-85	Nineteenth	20	Govt. Girls Sr. Sec. School, Moti Nagar, New Delhi.
20.	1985-86	Twentieth	29	Govt. Girls Sr. Sec. School, Jungpura, New Delhi.
21.	1986-87	Twenty-first	26	Govt. Girls Sr. Sec. School, Krishna Nagar, Delhi.
22.	1987-88	Twenty-second	27	Govt. Girls Sr. Sec. School, Vivek Vihar, Delhi.
23.	1988-89	Twenty-third	31	Govt. Girls Sr. Sec. School, No. 1, Lodhi Road, New Delhi.
24.	1989-90	Twenty-fourth	53	MB DAV Sr. Sec. School, Yusuf Sarai, New Delhi.
25.	1990-91	Twenty-fifth	29	Govt. Girls Sr. Sec. School, Palam Enclave, New Delhi.
26.	1991-92	Twenty-sixth	35	Govt. Girls Sr. Sec. School, GT, Road, Shahdara, Delhi.
27.	1992-93	Twenty-Seventh	48	Govt. Girls Sr. Sec. School, Adarsh Nagar, Delhi.
28.	]1993-94	Twenty-Eighth	41	Govt. Girls Sr. Sec. School No. 1, Sarojini Nagar, New Delhi.
29.	1994-95	Twenty-Ninth	50	Maharaja Agarsain Public School, Ashok Vihar, Phase-IV, Delhi.
30.	1995-96	Thirtieth	43	Maharaja Agarsain Public School, Ashok Vihar, Phase-IV, Delhi.
31.	1996-97	Thirty-first	54	Govt. Girls Sr. Sec. School, Andrews Ganj, New Delhi.
32.	1997-98	Thirty-second	53	Govt. Girls Sr. Sec. School No. 1, Kalkaji, New Delhi.
33.	1998-99	Thirty-third	53	Manav Sthali School, 'R' Block, New Rajinder Nagar, New Delhi.

(Contd. . .)

To broaden the base and reach of this activity, from the year 1995, the schools run by New Delhi Municipal Council were also brought under the ambit of Youth Parliament Scheme. This year 5 schools of NDMC participated in the competition.

Prize distribution function of 32nd youth parliament competition

The Prize Distribution Function of the 32nd Youth Parliament Competition was held on 6th August, 1998 in Mavalankar Auditorium, Rafi Marg, New Delhi. Shri Madan Lal Khurana, Hon'ble Minister of Parliamentary Affairs presided over the function and distributed the prizes.

On this occasion, Govt. Girls Sr. Sec. School No. 1, Kalkaji, New Delhi, which stood first in the Competition gave a repeat performance of their sitting of Youth Parliament.

The Motilal Nehru running Parliamentary Shield and a trophy for securing first position in the Competition among the Delhi Government Schools was awarded to Govt. Girls Sr. Sec. School No. 1, Kalkaji, New Delhi. N.P. Co-ed Sr. Sec. School, Ansari Nagar, New Delhi stood first among the New Entrants Schools for which, -it was awarded the 'New Entrants Trophy'. 13 Schools were awarded trophies for their meritorious performance in the Competition. Besides, individual merit prizes were awarded to 631 students from 53 schools for their outstanding performance. The District Trophy for the Best Education District in the Competition was awarded to the New Delhi Municipal Council District.

Thirty third youth parliament competition

Orientation course

An Orientation Course for the teachers-in-charge of participating schools was conducted by this Ministry on

31st July, 1998 in Parliament House. Necessary background material was distributed and explanatory lectures were delivered by the officers of the Ministry of Parliamentary Affairs and Directorate of Education, Government of NCT of Delhi. During the course, 74 teachers from 58 schools participated.

Competition

Thirty third Youth Parliament Competition, 1998-99 for Senior Secondary Schools of Directorate of Education, Government of NCT of Delhi and NDMC was held between 5.10.1998 to 11.12.1998, 53 schools participated in the Competition.

Little Flower Pusha School, Shivaji Park, Shahdara, Delhi was adjudged first among the New Entrant Schools. 13 Other Schools have been placed in the Merit List for their outstanding performance in the competition. The West Educational District, Directorate of Education, Govt. of NCT bagged the 'Best Educational' District award in the Competition,

Youth Parliament competition in Kendriya Vidyalayss

In the year 1978, Kendriya Vidyalayas located in and around Delhi were incorporated into the ongoing Youth Parliament Competition in: the Higher Secondary Schools under the Directorate of Education, Government of NCT of Delhi. Gradually, due to increase in the number of schools, in 1983, a separate scheme was launched for the Kendriya Vidyalayas in and around Delhi on lines similar to that of the scheme for Sr. Sec. Schools under the Directorate of Education, Govt. of NCT of Delhi.

In the year 1988, the Scheme of Youth Parliament was launched at the National level in Kendriya Vidyalayas, as a part of celebrations of Pandit Jawahar Lal Nehru Birth centenary and 40 years of India's Independence.

Details of the Youth Parliament Competitions held between 1983-88 among Kendriya Vidyalayas located in and around Delhi are given below:-

Sl. No.	Year	Number of Participating schools	Name of the school standing first
1.	1983-84	20	K.V. No. 1, AFS, Agra
2.	1984-85	20	K.V., INA Colony, -New Delhi
3.	1985-86	26	K.V., KCC, Khetri Nagar (Rajasthan)
4.	1986-87	26	K.V. No. 1, Gwalior (M.P.)
5.	1987-88	31	K.V., J.N.U. Campus, New Delhi

Details of the National Youth Parliament Competitions for the Kendriya Vidyalaya Sangathan initiated from 1988 are given below:-

Sl. No.	Year	Competition	No. of participating school	Vidyalaya which stood first at National level
1.	1988-89	First	71	K.V. No.1, AFS, Agra
2.	1989-90	Second	113	K.V. No.1, Imphal
3.	1990-91	Third	108	K.V., Kankar Bagh, Patna
4.	1991-92	Fourth	108	K.V. No. 2, Srivijayanagar, Visakhapatnam (A.P.)
5.	1992-93	Fifth	194	K.V. No.1, Ramnagar Area, Tirupati (A.P.)
6.	1993-94	Sixth	103	K.V., Koliwada, Mumbai
7.	1994-95	Seventh	132	K.V., Sector-J, Aliganj, Lucknow,
8.	1995-96	Eighth	131	K.V. No. 2, R.S. Colaba, New Navy Nagar, Mumbai
9.	1996-97	Ninth	176	K.V., Dogra Lines, Meerut Cantt. (U.P.)

(Contd..)

10.	1997-98	Tenth	172	K.V., Pithoragarh (U.P.)
11.	1998-99	Eleventh	192	K.V. No.1, Gwalior (M.P.)

Prize distribution function

The Prize Distribution Function of the Tenth National Youth Parliament Competition was held on 24th April, 1998 in Mavalankar Auditorium, Rafi Marg, New Delhi. Shri R.K. Kumar, Minister of State for Parliamentary Affairs presided over the function and gave away the prizes. Kendriya Vidyalaya, Pithoragarh (U.P.), which stood first in the Competition gave a repeat performance of their sitting of Youth Parliament. 5 Kendriya Vidyalayas were awarded Zonal First Trophies for their meritorious performance in their Zones and 13 Vidyalayas were - awarded Merit Trophies of their outstanding performance at Regional Level. Besides, 4 individual prizes were also awarded to students in each of the participating Kendriya Vidyalayas at Regional Level Competition.

A total of 216 students were awarded certificates and prizes for their meritorious performance at the Zonal and National Level at the Prize Distribution Function. The total number of students thus getting certificates and prizes was 886.

Eleventh national youth parliament competition

Orientation course

In order to make the Orientation Course more intensive and purposeful the Ministry in consultation with the Kendriya Vidyalaya Sangathan organised four separate courses in connection with the 11th National Youth Parliament Competition, 1998-99 as under:-

(1) First Orientation Course-held on 23rd and 24th June, 1998 at Kendriya Vidyalaya, Oil India Limited, Duliajan, Distt. Dibrugarh (Assam). The Course was inaugurated by Shri Bhattacharyajee, Chief Manager (Production), Oil India Limited, Duliajan, Assam. In

the Orientation Course, 1 Education Officer and 23 teachers from 4 regions i.e. Guwahati, Calcutta, Silchar and Patna participated.

(2) Second Orientation Course-held at Palampur, Himachal Pradesh on 29th & 30th June, 1998 at Kendriya Vidyalaya, Holta Camp, Palampur, Distt. Kangra-(H.P.). The Course was inaugurated by Brigd. A.C. Chopra, VSM Commender, 87-Mountain Bridge, Palampur Himachal Pradesh. In the Orientation Course 4 Education Officers and 57 teachers from 5 regions i.e. Delhi, Dehradun, Jammu, Lucknow and Chandigarh participated.

(3) Third Orientation Course-held at Ootacamund, The Nilgiris (Tamilnadu) on 6th & 7th July, 1998 at Kendriya Vidyalaya, Ootacantund, HPF, Indunagar, The Nilgiris (Tamilnadu). The Course was inaugurated by Shri I.D. Sharma, Deputy Secretary, Ministry of Parliamentary Affairs. In the Course 3 Education Officers and 49 teachers from 5 regions i.e. Chennai, Bangalore, Hyderabad, Jabalplur and Bhubaneswar participated.

(4) Fourth Orientation Course-held at Pune (Maharashtra) on 9th and 10th July, 1998 at Kendriya Vidyalaya, BEG & Centre, Deccan College Road, Yerwada, Near Sadal Baba, Pune (Maharashtra). The Course was inaugurated by Shri I.D. Sharma, Deputy Secretary, Ministry of Parliamentary Affairs. In the Orientation Course 4 Education Officers and 49 teachers from 5 regions i.e. Ahmedabad, Jaipur, Mumbai, Gwalior and Bhopal participated.

Competition

The Eleventh National Youth Parliament Competition, 1998-99 for Kendriya Vidyalayas was held between 24.9.1998 to 4.1.1999. 20 Vidyalayas participated at National Level and 172 Vidyalayas participated at the Regional Level in these competitions.

Kendriya Vidyalaya, No.1, Gwalior (M.P.) secured the first position in the competition.

Youth parliament competition—Jawahar Navodaya Vidyalayas

In the year 1997, the scheme of Youth Parliament was launched at the National Level in the Jawahar Navodaya Vidyalayas, as a part of celebration of Golden Jubilee year of India's Independence on the pattern of the National Scheme for the Kendriya Vidyalayas.

First National Youth Parliament Competition was held during 1997-98. 8 Jawahar Navodaya Vidyalayas participated in the National Level and 34 Vidyalayas participated at the Regional Level Competition. Jawahar Navodaya Vidyalaya, Kulamavu, Distt. Iddukki, Kerala secured first position in the Competition.

Prize distribution function of first national youth parliament competition

The Prize Distribution Function of the First National Youth Parliament Competition, 1997-98 was held on 29th April, 1998 in Mavalankar Auditorium, Rafi Marg, New Delhi. Shri Ram Naik, Minister of State for, Railways, Parliamentary Affairs and Planning and Programme Implementation presided over the function and gave away the prizes to the prize winning students and institutions. On this occasion the students of Jawahar Navodaya Vidyalaya, Kulamavu, District Iddukki, which stood first in the Competition, gave a repeat performance of their Youth Parliament Session. 7 Jawahar Navodaya Vidyalayas, were awarded 'Regional First' trophies for their meritorious performance in their regions. Besides, 4 individual prizes were also awarded to students from each participating Vidyalaya at regional level. The total number of 143 students were given prizes and certificates at the regional level competition.

A total of 127 students were given certificates and prizes for their meritorious performance at the National Level at the Prize Distribution Function. The total number of prize and certificate getting students was 240.

Second national youth parliament competition

Orientation course

In order to make the Orientation Course more intensive and purposeful the Ministry in consultation with Navodaya Vidyalaya Samiti organised two separate courses in connection with the 2nd National Youth Parliament Competition, 1998-99 as under:-

(1) First Orientation Course-held at New Delhi at National Council of Educational Research and Training Campus, Hauz Khas, New Delhi on 23rd and 24th July, 1998. The Course was inaugurated by Shri S.A.T. Rizvi, Secretary, Ministry of Parliamentary Affairs. In the Orientation Course, 4 Assistant Directors and 29 teachers from 4 regions i.e. Chandigarh, Shillong, Jaipur and Patna participated.

(2) Second Orientation Course—held at Hyderabad at Jawahar Navodaya Vidyalaya, Gachhibowli, Hyderabad (A.P.) on 3rd and 4th August, 1998. The Course was inaugurated by Shri D.R. Tiwari, Joint Secretary, Ministry of Parliamentary Affairs. In the Course 5 Assistant Directors and 32 teachers from 4 regions i.e. Bhopal, Hyderabad, Lucknow and Pune participated.

Competition

The Second National Youth Parliament Competition, 1998-99 for Jawahar Navodaya Vidyalayas was held.

Youth parliament competition in the universities/colleges

As a part of Celebrations of Golden Jubilee year of India's Independence, this Ministry has launched the scheme of Youth Parliament for the first time in the Universities/ Colleges all over the country with the cooperation of University Grants Commission and Association of Indian Universities during 1997-98. First National Youth Parliament Competition, 1997-98 for the Universities and Colleges was held among 13 Universities/Colleges from 23.12.97 to 25.3.98. Maharishi Dayanand University,

Rohtak, Haryana secured the first position in the Competition.

Prize distribution function of first national youth parliament competition

The Prize Distribution Function of the First National Youth Parliament Competition was held on 14th August, 1998 in Mavalankar Auditorium, Rafi Marg, New-Delhi. Shri Madan Lal Khurana, Hon'ble Minister of Parliamentary Affairs and Tourism presided over the function and distributed the prizes to the prize winning students/ institutions. On this occasion the students of Maharishi Dayanand University, Rohtak, Haryana gave a repeat performance of their prize winning Youth Parliament Session. 13 Universities/Colleges were awarded Merit Trophies for their meritorious performance.

A total of 138 students were awarded certificates and prizes for their outstanding performance in the competition.

Second national youth parliament competition

Orientation course

Ministry of Parliamentary Affairs held an Orientation Course for the benefit of organisers of Youth Parliament in participating Universities/Colleges at New Delhi on 5th, 6th and 7th November, 1998. The Course was inaugurated by Shri S.A.T Rizvi, Secretary, Ministry of Parliamentary Affairs on 5th November, 1998 in Committee Room No. 53, Parliament House, New Delhi. On 6th & 7th November, 1998, the Course was held at C.P.D.H.E. Hall, Delhi University, Delhi. 43 Co-ordinators from all participating universities/colleges participated in the Course.

Youth parliament competition in states./union territories

The Fourth All India Whips Conference had recommended for the introduction of the Youth Parliament Competition in the States/UTs all over the country. In pursuance of the above recommendation, Ministry of Parliamentary Affairs drew up a detailed Scheme of Mock Parliament (now 'Youth Parliament' Competitions') and decided to introduce it on an experimental basis in the Higher Secondary Schools of Delhi,

The Sixth and Seventh All India Whips' Conference held at Shimla in 1967 and at Madras in 1969 made the following recommendations respectively:—

> "While appreciating the work done by the Ministry of Parliamentary Affairs with regard to promotion of 'Youth Parliament' in Schools in Delhi, the Conference recommends very strongly that the States should also arrange to introduce the Scheme in their respective States (6th AIWC)."
>
> "Keeping in view the successful execution of the 'Mock Parliament' Scheme in Delhi schools, the wider appreciation it received from leading Parliamentarians, the Press and Educationists and with a view to build a strong Parliamentary, system in the country, the Conference strongly recommends that:—

(a) All the States/Union Territories should take steps to implement the Scheme in their respective States./ Union Territories on pattern adopted by the Central Ministry of Parliamentary Affairs;

(b) The Central Ministry of Parliamentary Affairs should provide all encouragement to the States/Union Territories for introducing the Scheme by offering financial assistance, if necessary; and

(c) The Central Ministry of Parliamentary Affairs should also organise inter-State competitions of the States/ Union Territories which have started implementation of the Scheme (7th AIWC)".

The above recommendations were subsequently reiterated in the Eighth, Ninth, Tenth and Eleventh All India Whips' Conferences. The Eleventh All India Whips' Conference had recommended as under:—

(a) The State Government/Union Territory Administrations which have not introduced the Scheme of 'Youth Parliament Competition in their States/Union Territories should take urgent step to introduce this Scheme on the pattern adopted by the Central Ministry of Parliamentary Affairs, for Schools in Delhi;

(b) The Central Ministry of Parliamentary Affairs should provide all encouragement to the State Government/ Union Territory Administrations for introducing/ implementing the Scheme by offering free literature, training and financial assistance upto Rs. 25,000/- per annum;

(c) Steps may be taken to introduce Youth Parliament Scheme in Colleges and Universities. The Conference also recommends that a subject for imparting education on Parliamentary matters may be introduced in colleges and universities to develop Parliamentary culture."

As per the latest information from the States/UTs, the Youth Parliament Scheme is being implemented in 22 States/UTs, detailed as under:

Arunachal Pradesh, Bihar, Goa, Delhi, Gujarat, Haryana, Himachal Pradesh, Madhya Pradesh, Maharashtra, Meghalaya, Mizoram, Orissa, Nagaland, Pondicherry, Punjab, Rajasthan, Tamilnadu, Tripura, Uttar Pradesh, West Bengal, Chandigarh, Dadra & Nagar Haveli.

Financial assistance to states/union territories

In view of the laudable objectives of the Scheme, the Seventh All India Whips' conference recommended that the Scheme should be extended to all the States/Union

Territories of the country and that the Ministry should give all possible help to encourage its implementation by offering financial assistance to the States and Union Territories which organise the Youth Parliament Competitions. Consequently a scheme of financial assistance was evolved by the Ministry in 1972-73, according to which, financial assistance upto a ceiling of Rs. 5,000/- was given to the States/Union Territories implementing the scheme to meet part of the expenditure incurred by them on awarding of prizes/certificates to the students/institutions for their meritorious performance in the competition.

During the year 1993, the ceiling of Financial Assistance to the States/Union Territories was raised to Rs. 10,000/-. As per the recommendations of the Eleventh All India Whips Conference, the ceiling of the financial assistance to the States/Union Territories was raised to Rs. 25,000/- with effect from 16.8.1996. As per the recommendation of the 12th All India Whips' Conference, a proposal to enhance the financial assistance to Rs. 2 lakhs has been sent to the Ministry of Finance for their concurrence. The Ministry of Finance have agreed to raise the ceiling of finance assistance to Rs. 1 lakh per annum.

Training for conducting youth parliament scheme is states/ union territories

The Ministry also provides necessary training and literature to give encouragement to the States/Union Territories in introducing the Scheme for the purpose, 'Orientation Courses' are conducted for the Principals, Teachers-in-charge and Organisers of such competitions in the States/Union Territories to give on-the-spot training in theory and practice of conducting 'Youth Parliament' competition.

11

Electoral Reforms

In 1990, a Committee headed by late Shri Dinesh Goswami made a number of proposals on electoral reforms. A number of recommendations of the Committee have since been given effect to with the enactment of the Chief Election Commissioner and other Election Commissioners (Conditions of Service) Act, 1991 and the Representation of the People (Amendment) Act, 1996. Recently, the Representation of the People (Amendment) Act, 1998 was enacted to amplify section 159 of the Representation of the People Act, 1951 to enable the Election Commission of India to deploy employees of public sector undertakings and autonomous bodies which are wholly or substantially funded by the Government, for election duties.

The United Front Government had identified a set of 24 proposals on electoral reforms. These proposals mainly consisted of unimplemented recommendations of the Dinesh Goswami Committee. That Government had also discussed those proposals with political parties in four meetings held in between August 1996 and July 1997. The United Front Government was also separately considering certain proposals for strengthening section 8 of the Representation of the People Act, 1951 to bar criminals from contesting elections. No final decision, however, could be taken by that Government in respect of any of those proposals.

The National Agenda for Governance of the present Government mandated introduction of necessary electoral reforms on the basis of the recommendations of Dinesh Goswami Committee and, accordingly, the present Government took up on priority basis consideration of unimplemented recommendations of Dinesh Goswami Committee. As the set of 24 proposals which was under consideration of previous Government mainly contained unimplemented recommendations of Dinesh Goswami Committee, at the initiative of the Home Minister, a meeting of leaders of various political parties was held on 22nd May, 1998 to discuss afresh those proposals. Pursuant to a decision taken at the said meeting, a High Powered Committee under the Chairmanship of Shri Indrajit Gupta, Member of Parliament, has been constituted to suggest concrete measures for providing State funding to recognized political parties. The Committee would also consider the related proposals pertaining to maintenance of accounts by political parties and audit thereof, ban on donations by companies to political parties, inclusion of expenses of political parties in the election expenses of candidates for the purposes of ceiling on election expenses and empowering of Election Commission of India to fix ceiling on election expenses before every general election.

The Election Commission of India has given its detailed views on the set of proposals which are presently being discussed with political parties. In addition, the Election Commission has also made certain other proposals. Proposals for strengthening Section 8 of the Representation of the People Act, 1951 to check criminals from contesting elections are as under:

(i) At present, while under sub-sections (2) and (3) of Section 8, a person gets disqualified from the date of his conviction and he continues to be disqualified for a further period of six years since his release, on the other hand, under sub section (1), a person is disqualified for a period of six years from the date of his conviction. It is proposed that in sub-section (1) also, the disqualification may start from the date of conviction and the person may continue to be disqualified for a further period of specified number of years since his release, to bring this sub-section in conformity with sub-sections (2) and (3). The Election Commission has recommended that the disqualification in all cases should start from the date of conviction and period of disqualification should be the period of sentence and an additional six years thereafter.

(ii) In sub sections (1) to (3) of section 8, the period of disqualification of the person may be enhanced from the existing six years to a suitable period. A person may be disqualified either for life or for a suitably enhanced period, say for fifteen years.

(iii) In sub section (3), the present period of 'not less than two years' be reduced to 'not less than one year' so that any person convicted for any offence and sentenced to imprisonment for not less than one year gets disqualified. This may cover most of the serious criminal offences. The Election Commission has recommended that clauses (2) and (3) of section 8 of the Representation of the People Act, 1951 be put together, simplified and the minimum sentence reduced from two years to six months.

(iv) Sub section (4) which at present provides that disqualification will not take effect in case of a person who on the date of the conviction is a Member of Parliament or the Legislature of a State till three months have elapsed from that date or, if within that period, an appeal or application for revision is brought in respect of the conviction or the sentence, until that appeal or application is disposed off by the Court, may be deleted so that all persons are brought within the ambit of Section 8.

(v) An explanation may be inserted to clarify that notwith standing the suspension of the conviction and release of convict on bail in an appeal to a higher court, the convicted person shall incur the disqualification provided in section 8 unless conviction itself is set aside in the appeal.

(vi) The nomination paper of a candidate may seek details of previous convictions/pending charges/ pending cases, etc. in respect of the candidate.

It is proposed to discuss aforesaid proposals for strengthening section 8, alongwith other proposals, in the next round of discussion with political parties which would be held after the report of the Indrajit Gupta Committee is received.

Members of Armed Forces have so far choice to vote either in person or through postal ballot. With the reduction in minimum campaign period from 20 days to 14 days, it was felt that to ensure full participation of members of armed forces etc. in electoral process, they may be provided facility to vote through proxy also. The Government has accordingly decided to give an additional choice to members of Armed Forces etc. to vote by proxy, if they so wish. The Election Laws (Amendment) Bill, 1998, to give effect to this decision, has already been introduced in Lok Sabha.

Features of the constitution (52nd Amendment) Act, 1985

The Tenth Schedule to the Constitution of India was incorporated by the Constitution (52nd Amendment) Act, 1985. It came into force w.e.f. 1.3.1985. The legislative intent behind the enactment was to curb and control the menace of crossing of the floor by the elected representatives of the people in legislatures. The broad outlines of the Anti-Defection law as contained in the 10th Schedule of the Constitution are summarised as follows:—

(1) A member would be disqualified for being a member of the House concerned if (a) he voluntarily gives up his membership of his political party and (b) if he votes or abstains from voting contrary to any direction (whip) issued by his political party without obtaining prior permission of the party or his voting or abstention had not been condoned within 15 days from the date of his voting.

(2) The Speaker or Chairman is made the arbitrator in deciding the question of disqualification under the law. (The provision to oust Court's jurisdiction in the matter has been struck down by the Supreme Court).

(3) The Provision would apply to independent members also.

(4) A nominated member who is not a member of any political party on the date of his nomination would be escaping disqualification only if he joins a political party before the expiry of six months.

(5) The provisions would not apply to members if they constitute a group representing a faction arising out of split provided the said group consists of not less than 1/3rd of the total membership of the legislature party.

(6) The provisions of disqualification would also not apply to members if they become members of a party brought about by merger of his original party and another party provided 2/3rd of the party agreed to such merger. This exemption would also apply to members who opted to function as a separate group not accepting the merger.

Under para (7) of the 10th Schedule there was a bar on jurisdiction of courts in respect of any matter connected with the disqualification of a member of a House. The. Supreme Court, however, in the case of Kihota Hollohon vs. Zachilhu and others by a majority judgement have struck down said para as invalid. The implications of the judgement is that the decisions of the Presiding Officer can be scrutinised by the Courts.

Demands have been made, from time to time, for strengthening the Anti-defection law on the ground that it has not been able to achieve the desired goal of checking defection. It has been criticised on the ground that it allows bulk defections while declaring individual defection as illegal. On the other hand, the law has also been criticised on the ground that it makes serious inroad into basic powers, privileges and immunities of members in regard to freedom of speech, freedom of action, which includes freedom of vote also.

12

Members of Parliament-Services Rendered

Salary and allowances

The Ministry is responsible for the administration of the following Acts of Parliament:-

1. The Salary, Allowances and Pension of Members of Parliament Act, 1954.
2. The Salaries and Allowances of Officers of Parliament Act, 1953;
3. The Salary and Allowances of Leaders of Opposition in Parliament Act, 1977; and
4. The Leaders and Chief Whips of Recognised Parties and Groups in Parliament (Facilities) Act, 1998.

Under Section 9 of the Salary, Allowances and Pension of Members of Parliament Act, 1954, a Joint Committee of both Houses of Parliament is constituted to make rules on matters specified under sub-section (3) thereof. Recommendations of the Joint Committee are processed in the Ministry in consultation with the Lok/Rajya Sabha Secretariats and the concerned Ministries/Departments. Action is taken to bring forward legislation, wherever necessary.

The Joint Committee on Salaries and Allowances of Members of Parliament constituted under section 9 of the

Salary, Allowances and Pension of Members of Parliament Act, 1954 and the Joint Parliamentary Committee set up under the Chairmanship of Shri A.R. Antulay, MP and subsequently under the Chairmanship of Shri K.P. Unnikrishnan, MP to suggest facilities and remuneration for Members of Parliament had made a number of recommendations for increasing the salary, allowances and facilities of Members of Parliament. After carefully considering these recommendations from the administrative, financial and legal feasibilities, some of these recommendations were accepted by the Government and the Salary, Allowances and Pension of Members of Parliament (Amendment) Bill, 1998 was introduced, considered and passed by both the Houses of Parliament on 4th August-, 1998 which was assented to by the President on 20th August, 1998 as Act 28 of 1998. The relevant Rules made under the Salary, Allowances and Pension of Members of Parliament Act, 1954 were amended to enhance certain facilities to Members of Parliament. The notifications to this effect were issued by the Lok Sabha Secretariat making them effective from 31.8.1998.

Keeping in view the proposal of Government to increase in the salary of the President of India from Rs. 20,000/- per month to Rs. 50,000/- per month, it was also decided to enhance the salary of the Vice-President, who is also the ex-office Chairman of the Council of States from the then existing salary of Rs. 7,500/- per month plus Daily Allowance @Rs. 200/- and Sumptuary Allowance of Rs. 1,000/- to a consolidated salary of Rs. 40,000/- per month. To give effect to this decision, the Salaries and Allowances of Officers of Parliament (Amendment) Bill, 1998 was introduced, considered and passed by the two Houses of Parliament on 4th August, 1998 which was assented to by the President as Act 20 of 1998 on 20th August, 1998.

Leaders and chief whips

The Eleventh All India Whips' Conference held at Bangalore in January, 1994 as well as the Twelfth All India Whips' Conference held at Srinagar in August, 1997 had recommended for extending certain facilities to the Whips of recognised parties in Parliament and State Legislatures.

The Smooth functioning of the Parliamentary system depends to a large extent, on the efficiency of the party machinery in the legislatures. The Chief Whips and Leaders of parties and groups in Parliament are important party functionaries who play a vital role in the proper functioning of the parties and groups in the legislatures and, hence, fulfil an important public purpose.

After due consideration of the matter as a whole and to implement the recommendations made by the All India Whips' Conferences in this regard in respect of the centre, the "Leaders and Chief Whips of Recognised Parties and Groups in Parliament (Facilities) Bill, 1998" was introduced in the Lok Sabha on 16.12.1998. The Bill was considered and passed by the Lok Sabha on 18.12.1998 and was also considered and passed by the Rajya Sabha on 21.12.1998. The Bill received the assent of the President of India on 7.1.1999.

The Bill provides for extending certain Secretariat and telephone facilities to the leaders and Chief Whips of the recognised parties and groups in both Houses of Parliament.

Welfare of members of parliament

In order to look after the needs of Members of Parliament admitted for treatment in hospitals, arrangements have been made with the leading hospitals in Delhi to obtain day-to-day information by telephone regarding hospitalisation of Members, followed by a report regarding the health condition of the Members admitted in the hospitals. The officials of the Ministry pay visits to the hospitals to enquire about the health condition of the Members and to render any assistance required by them. The Minister/Ministers of State and Senior officers also make courtesy calls on the Members admitted in hospitals.

In the unfortunate event of passing away of a Member of Parliament in Delhi, the Ministry of Parliamentary Affairs renders all necessary assistance to the bereaved family in taking the mortal remains of the deceased Members for last rites to a place chosen by the family.

Transport arrangement for members of parliament

The Ministry of Parliamentary Affairs looks after regular transportation arrangements for carrying the Members of Parliament from their residence to Parliament House and back. It also arranges DTC buses for the Members/Staff on duty on special hire, during the late, sitting of the House to enable them to reach their residences during odd hours in night.

In order to improve transportation service to MPs, Hon'ble Speaker had invited suggestions from Hon'ble Minister of Parliamentary Affairs. Accordingly Secretary, Ministry of Parliamentary Affairs held a series of meetings with senior officers of Delhi Transport Corporation and India Tourism Development Corporation seeking details, facts, figures and their experiences on this kind of transportation.

On 29.10.1998 Hon'ble Minister of Parliamentary Affairs held another meeting with senior -officers of DTC, ITDC, Lok Sabha and Rajya Sabha Secretariats and discussed the various proposals received from DTC and ITDC threadbare. After taking into account various relevant factors, it was unanimously decided that this responsibility may be entrusted to DTC. This was conveyed to Lok Sabha Secretariat for consideration by the House Committee and Hon'ble Speaker, Lok Sabha.

This Ministry makes arrangements for dinner/ refreshments to the Members of Parliament, Press and Staff on duty in Parliament House during the late sittings of the House(s). This Ministry also arranges transport facilities for Members of Parliament and Staff on duty to reach their homes at odd hours of night during late sitting of the House(s) of Parliament in coordination with the Delhi Transport Corporation. During the period under report dinners were arranged for the MPs etc. on seven occasions.

The other occasions when lunch/dinner were arranged:

(1) Minister of Parliamentary Affairs & Tourism hosted a lunch in honour of Leaders of all political parties in Parliament on 22.5.1998 at Parliament House Annexe after a meeting regarding Electoral Reforms.

(2) Minister of Parliamentary Affairs & Tourism hosted a dinner to Leaders of political parties in Parliament on 9.12.1998 at Parliament House Annexe after a meeting on Reservation of Women in Parliament and State Legislatures Bill.

This Ministry renders ushering service on important public functions in which Members of Parliament are invited. Such duties are required to be performed on Republic Day Parade, Beating Retreat Ceremonies etc.

Ministry of Parliamentary Affairs arranges screening of feature films in various languages for entertainment of Members of Parliament in coordination with the Ministry of Information and Broadcasting. The Ministry of Parliamentary Affairs rendered all necessary coordination/ assistance including Special Bus/Security arrangements, in connection with the shows.

13

Leaders/Whips of Opposition Parties/Groups

This Ministry makes necessary arrangements/Coordinates the meeting of various political parties in Parliament convened by Prime Minister, Minister of Parliamentary Affairs, Minister of Home Affairs. During the year under report the following meetings were held:

(1) On 22nd May, 1998, Minister of Parliamentary Affairs & Tourism convened a meeting with leaders of all political parties in Parliament for further discussion on Electoral Reforms. The Home Minister presided over the meeting. Minister of State for Railways and Minister of State for Law, Justice and Company Affairs were also present in the meeting.

(2) Minister of Parliamentary Affairs and Tourism convened a meeting with leaders of all political parties in Parliament on 10th July, 1998 to discuss the Constitution (84th Amendment) Bill relating to Reservation of Women in Lok Sabha and Legislative Assemblies in States. The Prime Minister presided over the meeting. The Minister of Home, Defence, Steel & Mines, Urban Affairs & Employment, Petroleum & Natural Gas, Law, Justice and Company Affairs and Tourism were also present in the meeting.

(3) Minister of Parliamentary Affairs & Tourism convened a meeting with leaders of all political parties in Parliament on 9th December, 1998 for consultation on the Women's Reservation Bill. The Prime Minister presided over the meeting. Minister of Home, Law, Justice and Company Affairs and Minister of State for Railways were also present in the meeting.

Meeting with chief whips

The Minister of Parliamentary Affairs holds meeting with the Chief Whips of various political parties/groups in Parliament during every session to discuss matters of mutual interest. During this year such meetings were held on 10th June, 1998, 3rd December, 1998 and 10th December, 1998.

Institute of whip and its functions

The efficient and smooth transaction of Parliamentary Business depends to a very large extent upon the office of the Whips who are responsible for efficiently carrying on the organisation of the parties inside Parliament. The Office of whip thus plays a key role in a Parliamentary democracy.

The duty of maintaining discipline and decorum in the House devolves upon the Speaker, the Leader of the House and the Leader(s) of the Opposition and Whips of political parties. The Minister of Parliamentary Affairs as Chief Whip of the ruling party in the Indian Parliament is responsible for the smooth conduct of business in the two Houses of Parliament along with other Parliamentary functionaries mentioned above.

Monitoring group of all India whips' conference

The Twelfth All India Whips' Conference held at Srinagar on 21st and 22nd August, 1997 had *inter-alia* recommended for setting up of a Monitoring Group consisting of Chief Whips of various political parties at the Centre and in the

States, under the Chairmanship of the Union Minister of Parliamentary Affairs, to watch the progress of implementation of the recommendations of the Twelfth All. India Whips' Conference and the views expressed in its Plenary Sessions.

In pursuance of the above recommendation of the Twelfth All India Whips' Conference a 16 member Monitoring Group under the Chairmanship of Shri Madan Lal Khurana, Union Minister of Parliamentary Affairs and Tourism was constituted on 17th July, 1998. Shri Ram Naik, Union Minister of State for Railways and Parliamentary Affairs was nominated as Vice-Chairman of the Monitoring Group.

In partial modification of the above notification another notification was issued on 13th October, 1998 nominating Shri Kanchi Pannerselvam, Member of Parliament who had subsequently been elected as Whip of the A.I.A.D.M.K party in Lok Sabha, as a member of the Monitoring Group in place of Shri S. Muregesan, Member of Parliament who had been originally nominated on the Monitoring Group vide the earlier notification dated 17th July, 1998.

Formation of sub-committees of monitoring group

At its first meeting held on 11th August, 1998 in New Delhi, the Monitoring Group decided to constitute two sub-committees for going to the various states to study and assess the stage of implementation of the recommendations of the Whips' Conference. The two sub-committees viz Sub-Committee 'A' and Sub-Committee 'B' are to cover the various States as indicated below:-

Sub-Committee 'A' – To cover Andhra Pradesh, Haryana, Himachal Pradesh, Karnataka, Kerala, Madhya Pradesh, Punjab, Rajasthan Tamilnadu, Uttar Pradesh, Delhi and Pondicherry.

Sub-Committee 'B'	–	To cover Assam, Arunachal Pradesh, Bihar, Goa, Gujarat Jammu & Kashmir, Maharashtra, Meghalaya, Manipur, Mizoram, Nagaland, Orissa, Sikkim, Tripura and West Bengal.

Sub-Committee 'B' of the Monitoring Group held its first meeting at Srinagar, Jammu & Kashmir on 22nd October, 1998. Sub-Committee 'A' held its first meeting at New Delhi on 22nd December, 1998.

14

Training Course in Parliamentary Procedures and Practices

Tarining for officers of ministries/departments

The Ministry organised the following one Orientation Course in Parliamentary Procedures and Practices for Officers of the Ministries/Departments of the Government of India during the year 1998:-

Designation of Officers who participated in the course partici- pated	No. of Officers	Duration of the Course
S.Os/Parl. Assistants/Assistants	28	9.11.98 to 11.11.98

Training for officers of state governments

In pursuance of recommendations of 10th and 11th All India Whips' Conferences, this Ministry has been organising Orientation Courses in Parliamentary Procedures and Practices for the officers of the level of Deputy Secretary/Under Secretary of the Parliamentary Legislative Affairs Departments of various States/Union Territories Administrations since 1994. During the period under Report, the following one course only was organised by the Ministry:—

States/U.Ts. who participated	No. of Officers	Duration of Course
For Officers of the Govt. of Uttar Pradesh	2	24.11.98 to 2.12.98

Training to parliamentary fellows

A batch of seven Parliamentary Fellows sponsored by the Institute of Constitutional and Parliamentary Studies, New Delhi received training in this Ministry from 16th March, 1998 to 20th March, 1998:-

1.	Mr. Mubarak Mohamed Razik	Srilanka
2.	Ms. A.A. Kulatalake	Srilanka
3.	Mr. Antwi Deckson	Ghana
4.	Miss Evelyn Brefo Boateng	Ghana
5.	Mr. Arshad H. Naqshibandi	India
6.	Shri Chiradeep Sen	India
7.	Shri Jyoti Prakash Mishra	India

15

Use of Hindi in the Ministry

For proper implementation of the Official Language Policy as well as provisions of the Official Language Act, 1963 and Rules made thereunder, there is Hindi Section in the Ministry.

In Pursuance of Rule 10(4) of Official Language Rules, 1976, the Ministry was notified on 5.1.1978 as an Office of Central Government whose staff has acquired working knowledge of Hindi. During the period under report, 4 employees were nominated for Hindi Typewriting training and one employee was nominated for Hindi language Training. All these employees have completed their training.

Under Section 3 (3) of Act, it is mandatory that both Hindi and English Version shall be used for certain purposes specified therein. Various sections of the Official Language Act also enjoin upon mandatory use of Hindi for certain purposes. To ensure that the papers are issued bilingually or in Hindi only, a check point has been set up in General Section (issue section).

To ensure that official Language Policy is properly implemented in the Ministry, an Official language Implementation Committee has been set up. During the - period under report, 3 meetings of the Implementation Committee were held on 18.6.98, 7.9.98 and 28.12.98 respectively.

To advise the Ministry on matters relating to the

progressive use of Hindi in official work and for implementation of the Official language Policy, there is a Hindi Salahkar Samiti in the Ministry. The tenure of last Committee was over on 24th August, 1997 and process for reconstitution of the new Committee is in progress.

'Hindi Fortnight' was celebrated in the Ministry from 1st September to 14th September, 1998. At the time of its inauguration, an appeal was made to the Officers and employees of the Ministry to do more and more work in Hindi. An inspection of all the Sections was carried out to assess the progress made in the use of Hindi in the Ministry. On the closing day of Hindi fortnight i.e. 14th September 1998, following incentive prizes were awarded to those employees who did more work in Hindi and to those employees also who participated in various on the spot competitions and won the prizes:-

(A) There is a Scheme of Government to award cash prizes to the employees for doing more work in Hindi during the year. Under this scheme, 2 employees, in the Ministry were awarded cash prizes. One employee was awarded 'First Prize' of Rs. 500/- and the other was awarded 'Second Prize' of Rs. 300/-

(B) During the Hindi fortnight, a noting and drafting competition in Hindi was organised on the spot. Under this scheme, five employees were awarded prizes in the form of books. First Prize was of Rs. 200/- second of Rs. 150/- third of Rs. 100/- and two consolation prizes were of Rs. 75/- each.

(C) From this year, Hindi Typing competition was also introduced in the Ministry. This Hindi Typing Competition was organised on the spot during the Hindi Fortnight. In this Competition, 4 employees were awarded prizes. First prize was of Rs. 100/- Second prize of Rs. 75/- and the third prize was of Rs. 50/-. Two employees were awarded first and Second Prize respectively and the other two were awarded Third Prize each.

There are 12 Sections in the Ministry. Out of which, 4 sections are doing cent-percent work in Hindi. Rest of the 9 sections are doing 25% to, 759/6 work in, Hindi. Accordingly, the percentage of work in Hindi in all the twelve section; s, of the Ministry is as under:-

1.	General Section	100%
2.	Implementation I Section	100%
3.	Implementation 11 Section	100%
4.	Hindi Section	100%
5.	Admn. Section	75%
6.	Legislative II Section	75%
7.	R&C Section	50%
8.	Welfare Section	50%
9.	Committee Section	50%
10.	Legislative I Section	25%
11.	Work Study Section	25%
12.	IFC Section	25%

During the year 1996-97, the Ministry organised a scheme of giving awards for writing original books in Hindi. The aim of this scheme was to encourage writing of original books in Hindi on the prescribed subject i.e. "Role of Opposition in Parliamentary Democracy". During the period under report, after evaluation of all the books received under the scheme, three writers were awarded cash prizes on 14th Sept., 1998 by the Hon'ble Minister of Parliamentary Affairs & Tourism in a function organised by the Ministry. These prizes were of Rs. 15,000/- First Prize, Rs. 10,000/- Second Prize and Rs. 5,0001- Third Prize.

The Ministry organised an All India Hindi Essay Competition during the year 1997. The aim of the competition was to arouse the interest of public in Parliamentary Democracy and to encourage writing on the subject in Hindi. The subject for the Essay Competition was "Cultural Integrity of India-Feasibility and Means". For this competition, an advertisement was given in the leading Newspapers. After evaluation of the essays received, 12 writers (8 from Region-1, 2-2 each from Region II and III) were selected for awarding prizes for their essays. These writers were awarded cash prizes, shield and a certificate by the Hon'ble Minister for Parliamentary Affairs & Tourism in a Prize Distribution Function which was organised on the Hindi Day i.e. 14th Sept., 1998.

To encourage the use of Hindi in the Ministry, two Hindi Workshops were organised during the period under report viz. first from 26th Feb. to 6th March, 1998 and the second from 2nd Sept. to 11th Sept., 1998. In these workshops, 20 employees were imparted training on noting and drafting in Hindi.

16

General

Leader of the Lok Sabha

Shri Atal Bihari Vajpayee is the Leader of the. Lok Sabha with effect from 19 March, 1998.

Leader of the Rajya Sabha

Shri Sikander Bakht, Minister of Industry is the Leader of the Rajya Sabha with effect from 21 March, 1998.

Leader of Opposition in the Lok Sabha

Shri Sharad Pawar, Leader of the Congress(I) Party in the Lok Sabha is the Leader of the Opposition with effect from 19 March, 1998.

Leader of Opposition in the Rajya Sabha

Dr. Manmohan Singh, Leader of the Congress (1) Party in the Rajya Sabha is the Leader of Opposition with effect from 21 March, 1998.

Deputy Speaker Elected

On 17 December, 1998, Shri P. M. Sayeed, a sitting member of the Lok Sabha was chosen as the Deputy Speaker of Lok Sabha on a motion moved by Shri Atal Bihari Vajpayee and seconded by Shri Sharad Pawar.

Work study

As per instructions of Government, Work Study Section functions in the Ministry for conducting work measurement and method/procedural studies of various sections and on various subject; coordinating action regarding such studies by the S.I.U. in Ministry of Finance and also to see that instructions issued from time to time in regard to proper custody, care and management of office records and other aspects of 0 & M are scrupulously followed in the Ministry.

Under Secretary (Work Study) has been authorised for evaluation and downgrading the classified records of the Ministry.

Section Officer (Work Study) has been nominated as Departmental Record Officer and also been entrusted the functions of Departmental Record Room in the Ministry.

Record Retention Schedule in respect of the Substantive functions of this Ministry was reviewed in consultation with representatives of National Archives of India who made on-the-spot study by visiting this. Ministry and revised accordingly was circulated for information and compliance in the Ministry.

Research work

This Ministry provides advice/technical guidance on matters of Parliamentary procedure and practice to central Ministries/Departments and State/Union Territory Governments whenever the same is asked for. From time to time, notes and brochures are prepared on various parliamentary and constitutional matters for official use.

Reservation for Scheduled Castes, Scheduled Tribes and other backward classes

The Ministry follows the instructions issued by the Government of India from time to time regarding reservation of vacancies for the Scheduled Castes, Scheduled Tribes and other Backward Classes.

Out of the total number of 140 employees (excluding the personal staff of Ministers) of the Ministry, 30 belong to the Scheduled Castes, 16 belong to the Scheduled Tribes -and 7 belong to Other Backward Class".

Budgetary position

The Budgetary Position of Ministry of Parliamentary Affairs is as under:-

(Amount in lakhs of Rupees)

Major Head Estimates 1998-99	Head Estimates 1998-99		Budget Estimates 1999-2000	Revised	Budget
Major Head "2052" Secretariat General Services 00.900 Secretariat (Minor Head) 13 Ministry of Parliamentary Affairs					
	13.00.01	Salaries	180.00	170.00	180.00
	13.00.03	Overtime Allowance	5.00	7.00	6.00
	13.00.11	Domestic Travel Expenses	9.00	9.00	10.00
	13.00.12	Foreign Travel Expenses	60.00	60.00	80.00
	13.00.13	Office Expenses	80.00	89.00	90.00
	13.00.16	Publications	4.00	7.00	6.00
	13.00.10	Other Administrative Expenses	50.00	30.00	40.00
	13.00.50	Other Charges	30.00	36.00	70.00

17

Indian Democracy

Our country is a Union of States, and a Socialist Secular Democratic Republic with a parliamentary system of government. India is governed in terms of the Constitution, which was adopted by Const-ituent Assembly on 26 November, 1949 and came into force on 26 January, 1950.The Constitution which evisages parliamentary from of government is federal in structure with unitary features.

President of India is constitutional head of executive of the Union. Article 74(1) of the Constitution provides that there shall be a Council of Ministers with the Prime Minister as head to aid and advise president who shall, in exercise of his functions, act in accordance with such advice. Real executive power thus vests in Council of Ministers with Prime minister as head. Council of Ministers is collectively responsible to the House of the People (Lok Sabha).

Similarly, in states, Governor is head of executive, but it is the Council of Ministers with Chief Minister as head in whom real executive power vests. Council of Ministers of a state is collectively responsible to Legislative Assembly. The Constitution distributes legislative power between Parliament and state legislatures and provides for vesting of residual powers in Parliament.

The union and its territory

India comprises 25 states and seven union territories. States are: Andhra Pradesh, Assam, Arunachal Pradesh, Bihar, Goa, Gujraat, Haryana, himachal Pradesh, Jammu and Kashmir, Karnataka, Kerala, Madhya Pradesh, Maharashtra, Manipur, Megthalaya, Mizoram, Nagaland, Orissa, Punjab, Rajasthan, Sikkim, Tamil Nadu, Tripura, Uttar Pradesh and West Bengal. Union territories are: Andaman and Nicobar Islands, Chandigarh, Dadra and Nagar Haveli, Daman and Diu, Delhi, Lakshadweep and Pondicherry.

The Constitution of India provides for a single and uniform citizenship for whole of India. Every person who was at commencement of the Constitution (26 January 1950) domiciled in the territory of India and: (a) who was born in the territory of India or (b) either of whose parents was born in the territory of India or (c) who has been ordinarily resident in the territory of India for not less than five years immediately preceding such commencement, shall be a citizen of India. The Citizenship Act, 1955 provides for acquisition and termination of citizenship after the commencement of the Constitution.

The Constitution offers all citizens, individually and collectively, some basic freedoms. These are guaranteed in the Constitution in the form of six broad categories of Fundamental Rights which are justiceable. Article 12 to 35 contained in Part III of the Constitution deal with Fundamental Rights. These are: (i) right to equality including equality before law, prohibition of discrimination on grounds of religion, race, caste, sex or place of birth and equality of opportunity in matters of employment; (ii) right to freedom of speech and expression; assembly; association or union; movement; residence; and right to practice any profession or occupation (some of these rights are subject to security of the State, friendly relations with foreign countries, public order, decency or morality); (iii) right against exploitation, prohibiting all forms of forced labour, child labour and traffic in human beings; (iv) right to freedom of conscience and free profession, practice and propagation of religion; (v) right of any section of citizens to conserve their culture, language or script and right of minorities to establish and administer educational institutions of their choice, and (vi) right to constitutional remedies for enforcement of Fundamental Rights.

By the 42nd Amendment of the Constitution, adopted in 1976, Fundamental Duties of the citizens have also been enumerated. Article 51 'A' contained in Part IV A of the Constitution deals with Fundamental Duties. These enjoin upon a citizen among other things, to abide by the Constitution, to cherish and follow noble ideals which inspired our national struggle for freedom, to defend the country and render national service when called upon to do so and to promote harmony and spirit of common brotherhood amongst all people of India transcending religious, linguistic and regional or sectional diversities.

The Constitution lays down certain Directive Principles of State Policy which though not justiceable, are 'fundamental in governance of the country' and it is 'the duty of the State to apply these principles in making laws'. These lay down that the State shall strive to promote welfare of people by securing and protecting as effectively as it may a social order in which justice–social, economic and political, shall inform all institutions of national life. The State shall direct its policy in such a manner as to secure the right of all men and women to an adequate means of livelihood, equal pay for equal work and within limits of its economic capacity and development, to make effective provision for securing the right to work, education and to public assistance in the event of unemployment, old age, sickness and disablement or other cases of undeserved want. The State shall also endeavour to secure to workers a living wage, humane conditions of work, a decent standard of life and full involvement of workers in management of industries.

In economic sphere, the State is to direct its policy in such a manner as to secure distribution of ownership and control of material resources of community to subserve the common good and to ensure that operation of economic system does not result in concentration of wealth and means of production to common detriment.

Some of the other important directives relate to provisions of opportunities and facilities for children to develop in a healthy manner, free and compulsory education for all children up to the age of 14; promotion of educational and economic interests of scheduled castes, scheduled tribes and other weaker sections; organisation of village panchayats; separation of judiciary from executive, promulgation of a uniform civil code for whole country; protection of national monuments; promotion of justice on a basis of equal opportunity; provision of free legal aid; protection and improvement of environment and safeguarding of forests and wildlife of the country and promotion of international peace and security, just and honourable relations between nations, respect for international law, treaty obligations and settlement of international disputes by arbitration.

The Indian Constitution is a remarkable document as it strikes a balance between tradition and modernity, between a federal structure and a strong centre and between the demands of social justice and the rights of the individual. However, as we enter the 50th year of our Independence, perhaps it would be desirable to take a close second look at the Constitution with a view to removing possible distortions and streamlining its functioning, feel the author.

Democracy is often described as government of the people, by the people and for the people. The Constitution, written as in the United States and other countries or unwritten but dependent on tradition as in the United Kingdom, lays down the framework for this form of government. But written or unwritten, there is a remarkable similarity between the two. In the United Kingdom the centre of power shifted first from the Crown to the nobles and then to the House of Commons. In the United States, judicial pronouncements have changed the complexion of the government. The federal Government has far more powers than was envisaged at first. All this was achieved by a process of evolution either by consensus as in the U.K. or by judicial pronouncements as it came up and a solution was found.

India became independent on August 15, 1947 and the Founding Fathers worked post haste to give the nation a new Constitution. The constitution was adopted by the Constitutent Assembly on November 26, 1949 and came into force on January 26, 1950. It was a remarkable achievement because many countries which became independent along with India were still floundering and trying to find their way in framing the Constitution. Countries, which became independent later, were looking at India's efforts. The Indian Constitution is a remarkable document as it strikes a balance between tradition and modernity, between a federal structure and strong centre between the demands of social justice and the rights of the individual and between conflicting demands in other areas.

Though the Founding Fathers were proud of the Constitution they had framed, they were also aware of their own limitations. As people move into a new house, they notice defects which had escaped the architect. Also conditions change and needs grow. Similarly, defects come to light as a Constitution comes into operation. Changes therefore become necessary and have to be made quickly and easily. As Dr. B.R. Ambedkar, the Law Minister, said on the day the Constitution was adopted, "The Assembly has not only refrained from putting a seal of finality and infallibility upon the Constitution by denying the people the right to amend the Constitution or making the amendment of the Constitution subject to the fulfilment of extraordinary terms and conditions, as in America or in Australia but has provided a more facile procedure foramending the Constitution". The President of the Constituent Assembly Dr. Rajendra Prasad observed "another important feature of the Constitution is that it enables amendments to be made without much difficulty".

Prime Minister Jawaharlal Nehru was even more forthright. Speaking on the first amendment made in 1951 he said, "People must realise that this great Constitution of ours, which we laboured for so long, is not a final or rigid thing which must either be accepted or broken. A Constitution which is responsive to their ideas, in that it can be revised here and there, they will respect it all the more and they will not fight against it. Otherwise if you make them feel that it is unchangeable and cannot be touched the only thing that can be done by people who wish to change it, is to try and break it. That is a dangerous thing and a bad thing. Therefore it is a desirable and a good thing for people to realise that this very fine Constitution which we have fashioned is good in so far as it goes but as society changes, as conditions change, we mend it in the proper way".

The members of the Constituent Assembly were conscious that they had been elected by members ofthe

Provincial Assemblies who had themselves been elected on a limited franchise. How could they put restrictions on the House of the People which was to be set up on the principle of universal adult franchise ? The leaders were also aware that in the years to come, conditions would change, new demands would be made and met and it would be the duty of the new rulers to meet the challenges as they came up. It was therefore that they left the way open for easy amendments without going through the arduous process of forming a new Constituent Assembly.

Events proved that the Founding Fathers of the Constitution showed robust common sense when they decided that the process of amending the Constitution should be easy. The first amendment was made in 1951 to make it possible among other things to carry out land reforms and abolish the zamindaris. Also, it was decided that reasonable restrictions could be placed on the exercise of Fundamental Rights in the interests of society. Since then, the Constitution has been amended more than 75 times. Most of these amendments were made to remove difficulties in the working of the Constitution, but others like the one about Panchayati Raj and Municipalities gave an entirely new dimension to administration by devolution of powers to local self-government bodies. The amendment about reservation for women in legislative bodies will add one more dimension to the Constitution.

The result is that the Constitution today resembles an ancient edifice to which additions and modifications have been made from time to time to suit the needs but in the process, the character of the original structure has been changed beyond recognition. Some of the provisions of the Constitution like introducing prohibition or banning cow slaughter have been found to be impossible to implement. Others like drafting a Common Civil Code have met with stiff opposition form sections of society. Similarly many of the Directive Principles of State Policy have been reduced to mere expression of pious intentions.

The Constituent Assembly utilised the period between August 15, 1947 and November 26, 1949 to draft the Constitution which came into force on January 26, 1950. On August 15 1997 India completes fifty years of Independence. It will be in the fitness of things if the task of taking a second look at the Constitution is attempted so as to remove the cobwebs and to streamline the working. A Committee of Parliament can undertake the job with inputs from politicians, experts in constitutional law, academics and journalists. The changes can be made by the time the nation celebrates the 50th anniversary of the enforcement of the Constitution and the establishment of the Indian Republic.

The paths to peace and freedom and equal rights were strewn with throrns and hurdles were placed at all steps. The White rule became a blot on the world conscience. Denial to right to live brought an upsurge among the Black South Africans. In their struggle, they found India and the Indians settled there as a great sorce of inspiration. It was not because Mahatma Gandhi's association with South Africa in the initial years of his political life that made India so receptive to the aspirations of the Black South Africans.

Perhaps in the South African freedom movement and struglle for equality was seen the same psyche of the Indian people who suffered humiliation, imprisonment and torture in India during the ong independence struggle. Indians felt genuinely for the Black South Africans. So did the government.

In less than a decade's existence as an independent nation, India brought before the world a new concept of governance based on the principle of "Panchsheel". It was but natural for a country that has a long tradition of tolerance. India with numerous languages and multiplicity of religion itself symbolises co-existence. Mutual respect for each other, irrespective of differences, demonstrates Indian ethos.

It is in this context, the Bandung conference in April 1955 that adopted "Panchsheel" created a new concept for the world already handed over to violence and turmoil. The Bandung conference had five proponents: India, Indonasia, Burma, Sri Lanka and Pakistan. The Bandung conference was preceded by the bombing ofthe Air India plane carrying delegates and journalists over South China sea. Evidently, forces that wanted the settlement of disputes through terrorism asserted their right to show their way of solving issue and problems.

India as a peace loving nation made its mark as a peacekeeper under the leadership of the United Nations. Peacekeeper's role came to India primarily because of its sense of fairness, coupled with the Indian armed forces' record of efficient functioning in warlike situationss. More than that, Nehru's approach usually proceeded on the assumption that peace cannot be promoted by creating positons of strength. On the contrary, the creation of positions of strength might become a threat to peace for every party will try to increase naturally its strength vis-s-vis its competitors for power, and such an attempt is bound to be counter productive, apart from being suicidal. It was Nehru's considered view that a deliberate policy of friendship with other countries goes further in gaining security than almost anything else. But in his Lifetime China proved it wrong when it attacked India in 1962.

India was involved in the Korean crisis within a few months of gaining Independence. After the Korean issue was brought before the Unied Nations in 1947, K.P.S. Menon was designated as the chairman of the first United Nations Temporary Commission on Korea. Ever since India was connected with the deliberations concerning the Korean peninsula, gearing its efforts towards reuniting the two halves of the nation. Unfortunately, even after 50 years the situation in Korea remains the same as before. It became a victim of cold war situation with foreign forces still operating on the South Korean soil.

In 1948, India once again headed the second United Nations Commission on Korea in June 1950, India's involvement was not confined only to the four corners ofthe U.N. Subsequently, India wa selected to be the chairman of the Neutral Nations Repatriation Commission that supervised the return of the prisoners of war to their respective countries. India devised a formula to solve the repatriation problem.

India's resolution at the General Assembly in the United nations formed the basis of the Armistice Agreement on December 3, 1952. When cease-fire was effected in Korea, the Custodian Force of India (CFI) took over the work of repatriation of POWs. In his report, Major General S.P.P. Throat has said force was not used for the purpose of taking out prisoners of war for explanations, while the CFI found that more than 90 per cent of the prisoners were anti-communist. Only 4 per cent of POWs were procommunist.

Over the past 35 years, India was called upon by the United Nations on many occasions to undertake peacekeeping work in various parts of the world. The most important among them may be mentioned as India's peacekeeping role in Gaza after the Arab-Israel war in 1967 and in the Congo operations. Between 1948 and June 30, 1994, over 650,000 military personnel have served in the UN peacekeeping force. Form the average of 300 million dollars expenditure on peacekeeping, it went up to 640 million in 1989. In 1994, the budget peaked to 3.8 billion dollars.

Indian forces found their active role in restoring peace in Cambodia, Mozambique and Somalia. In all these operations, Indian forces acquitted themselves creditably.

There is no doubt that India will continue to play an important role in the Un peacekeeping in the future. For an enhanced and effective role, India needs to set up a necessaty organisation which could be set in motion quickly. Given the emerging world order, instability and conflict will be a recurring phenomenon inthe decades to come.

Politicians will try to shy away from the task on the ground that it will mean opening a Pandora's box, which it will certainly be. The States will demand more powers even autonomy, while some will ask for more powers for the centre. Conflicting claims and demands will be made. Should we have directive Principles of State Policy which cannot be enforced in a Court of Law? All these and more will have to be looked into.

But there are some problems which cannot be pushed under the carpet any more. When the Constitution was framed, the Assembly had to a large extent placed before itself the Westminster form of Government. In such a form of government, two political parties vie for power. There is a general agreement on basic problems and policies. The Founding Fathers had possibly hoped that in course of time in India also, two rival parties would emerge. But this has not happened. We have a plethora of political parties. Three successive elections to the Lok Sabha did not give any political party a clear majority. Even when a politial party has the majority, its leader is always worried about keeping his flock together. Policies are often framed not so much for national good but for narrow political ends.

But what is the remedy if the electorate does not give a clear verdict in election after electon? The Constitution has no provision for direct rule by the President at the Centre because this might result insubversion of democracy and the establishment of a dictatorship. At the State level, the Constitution provides for imposition of President's rule. Dr. Ambedkar had expressed the hope that his provision might never be used. Events have proved otherwise and in the last 47 years, it has been used more than 100 times. There is justification for doing so when separatist forces and militancy pose threat to democracy as in Punjab, Jammu & Kashmir and Assam but no justificaton when it is used for political purposes.

But what is the way out at the Centre or in the States if no party gets a clear majority in election after election? A poor country can ill afford the luxury of election after election without a verdict in favour of any single party. Students and scholars of political science and leaders of political parties have been worried about this for a long time. Even during the days of Mrs. Indira Gandhi a suggestion was made that India should go in for a presidential form of government. The former Union Minister and senior parliamentarian Mr. Vasant Sathe has long been advocating this and has also said that this change can be made with a few changes in the Constitution.

There is another area where the distortion is worsening every day. Under the original scheme of things, a population of 7½ lakh elected a member of the Lok Sabha. The first Lok Sabha thus had 489 elected members. The Constitution also provided that the number of seats would go up according to the figures of population in the previous census. The seats went up to 545 by 1976. But it was felt that the increase gave an unfair advantage to the States which did not take up the family planning programme in earnest. Therefore, the number of seats in the Lok Sabha and in the Assemblies was frozen at the figures of 1976. By an amendment of the Constitution it was decided that the readjustment ofseats on the basis of population would be made only after the figures of the first census after the year 2000 were publidhed. The next Lok Sabha election would be held in 2001 which is also the year in which the next census will be held. By then the figures of the census are not likely to be available. But a serious thought will have to be given now to the question of the ratio between the population and the number of seats in the Lok Sabha and the State Assemblies. If the original scheme of one Lok Sabha member for every 7.50 lakh population were to be followed the Lok Sabha todays should have a membership of more than 1300. By the turn of the century the population of India is likely to go up to 100 crore and the membership of the Lok Sabha would have to be more than 1400. The Uttar pradesh Assembly would similiarly have a strength of 800 today. It will be impossible to manage such a large House.

But then if this is not done, the Lok Sabha constituencies would be so large in terms of population that it will be impossible for a candidate to contact the voters and for a candidate to contact the voters and for the M.P. to maintain contacts with his constituency. Outer Delhi today has electorate of nearly 30 lakh. Thane in Maharashtra comes a close second with an electorate of 26 lakh. It is well nigh impossible for anyone to claim that he can look after the interests of such a large electorate much less to visit the distant areas regularly. Many constituencies of the U.P. Assembly today have the same electorate as the Lok Sabha had in 1952. A fresh delimitation can only solve the problem partially. What is needed is a fresh look and a new initiative.

Under the present system the candidate who gets the largest number of votes is declared elected. Frequently the combined votes of the other candidates are more than his votes. It has also happened that a political party might get a majority of the seats. A swing of a mere 5 per cent can make a tremendous difference. Any review of the Constitution must look at this anomaly and find ways to remove it.

The Union executive consists of President, Vice President and Council of Ministers with Prime Minister at the head to aid and advice President.

President is elected by members of an electoral college consisting of elected members of both House of Parliament and Legislative Assumblies of the states in accordance with the system of proportional representation by means of single transferable vote. To secure uniformity among states *inter se* as well as parity between the states, as a whole, and the Union, suitable weightage is given to each vote. President must be a citizen of India, not less than 35 years of age and qualified for election as member of the Lok Sabha. His term of office is five years and he is eligible for re-election. His removal from office is to be in accordance with procedure prescribed in Article 61 of the Constitution. (He may, by writing under his hand addressed to Vice President, resign his office.)

Executive power of the Union is vested in President and is exercised by him either directly or through officers subordinate to him in accordance with the Constitution. Supreme Command of defence forces of the Union also vests in him.

President summons, prorogues, addresses, sends messages to Parliament and dissolves the Lok Sabha; promulgates Ordinances at any time, except when both Houses of Parliament are in session; makes recommendations for introducing financial and money bills and gives assent to bills; grants pardons, reprieves, respites or remissions of punishment or suspends, remits or commutes sentences in certain cases. When there is a failure of the constitutional machinery in a state, he can assume to hmself all or any of the functions of the government of that state. President can proclaim emergency in the country if he is satisfied that a grave emergency exists whereby security of India or any part of its territory is threatened whether by war or external aggression or armed rebellion.

Vice president

Vice President is elected by members of an electoral college consisting of members of both Houses of Parliament in accordance with the system of proportional representation by means of single transferable vote. He must be a citizen of India, not less than 35 years of age and eligible for election as a member of the Rajya Sabha. His term of office is five years and he is eligible for re-election. His removal from office is to be in accordance with procudure prescribed in Article 67 b.

Vice Presidents is *ex-offico* Chairman of the Rajya Sabha and acts as President when the latter is unable to discharge his functions due to absence, illness or any other cause or till the election of a new President (to be held within six months) when a vacancy is caused by death, resignation or removal or otherwise of President. While so acting, he ceases to perform the function of the Chairman of the Rajya Sabha.

There is a Council of Ministers headed by PrimeMinister to aid and advise President in exercise of his functions. Prime Minister is appointed by President who also appoints other ministers on the advice of Prime Minister. The Council is collectively responsible to the Lok Sabha. It is the duty of the Prime Minister to communicate to President all decisions of Council of Ministers relating to administeration of affairs of the Union and proposals for legislation and information relating to them.

The Council of Ministers comprises Ministers who members of Cabinet, Ministers of State (independent charge), Ministers of State and Deputy Ministers.

Legislature of the Union which is called Parliament, consists of President and two Houses, known as Council of States (Rajya Sabha) and House of the People (Lok Sabha). Each House of Parliament has to meet within six months of its previous sitting. A joint sitting of two Houses can be held in certain cases.

A switch over to the Presidential Form of Government will be a far reaching change which can only be made after a nation wide debate. But the immediate problems of the electoral system need to be examined quickly. A 'hung' Lok Sabha or State Assembly leads to defections and politics of expendiency and negates democracy. We have to find an answer to it. Introduction of proportional representation is not prctical in a large country like India. But should we then have a system of direct election for half the seats and proportional representation for the other half? This experiment has been tried succesfully in Japan.

Another area for attention is the role of the Rajya Sabha and the Legislative Councils in some States. These were envisaged as chambers of revision but over the years have largely become chambers where the work is mostly duplicated. Our Rajya Sabha is neither as powerful as the Senate in the USA nor powerless as the

House of Lords in the U.K. Its powers and functioning deserve a close second look. Unlike the Lok Sabha, the Rajya Sabha is supposed to represent the States. It has therefore been laid down that its members should be normally resident in the State from which they are elected. But more and more instances come up where he does not live. It is easy to look at this as a technical violation of the Constitution. But another aspect is often overlooked. States like Punjab and Jammu & Kashmir were for long years been under President's rule and the Legislative Assemblies had been dissolved and could not elect members to the Rajya Sabha, elections to the Lok Sabha were also not held there. Should the people of these States be denied the right of representation at both the Central and State levels for no fault of their own? Election tot he Rajya Sabha from another state might not be strictly according to the letter of the Constitution but it at least gives a politician from such a State to put forward the views of the people and to air their grievances.

It is well known that militancy in Punjab was limited to a few districts and in Jammu & Kashmir to the Kashmir Valley. But since the Assembly had been dissolved and the State placed under Central rule, areas where there was comparative peace could also not go to the polls even for the Lok Sabha. They were penalised for no faults of theirs. Any review of the Constitution has to consider this question and find a solution.

It is to the credit of India that while other countries which became independent along with her have had long periods of dictatorship or military rule, democracy has continued to grow in India. The Indian voter has been no respecter of men and has not hesitated to throw out powerful leaders if he found that they were not performing well. The base has widened with the devolution of powers to the local self-governing bodies. The proposal to reserve seats for women in legislative bodies is proof of the fact that political parties forget their differences on giving greater powers to the neglected segments of society. Changes have been made in the Constitution to keep pace with the times.

As India enters the 50th year of her Independence it is time to do a soul searching and to examine whether the Constitution needs a close second look so as to remove the cobwebs and to remove the distortions and discrepancies.

If the Plan objectives and programmes are to be translated into reality, the close co-operation and co-ordination from the States is ess-ential. The economic reform programmes which form a guide-post of the Central direction could succeed only if the States are sincere and committed to the cause. Much of the benefits of direct investment depends on the policy and initiative of the State governments. Reforms can receive greater acceptability only if poverty alleviation measures are implemented vigorously, which has to be done by the States. The development of infrastructure and social sector has ultimately to be implemented by the States.

We have already noted that a vital constraint of growth and development is unchecked population. The family welfare programmes and population control mechanism are in the hands of State governments. Statistics show that some States have advanced in the direction while others are lagging behind. The story of success or failure in this direction has been caused by the extent to which the States are sincere and devoted to the cause. The newly revamped public distribution system of the deva Gowda government has decided to supply 10 kg of food grains at half the PDS price to 60 million families below the poverty line "in order that nobody could complain about the step as the aim was to benefit the poor." It may be recalled that during the Food

Ministers' conference at New Delhi in August 1996, the State Food Ministers refused to withdraw the PDS benefits from affluent classes and also to raise the price of ration items. Again, the identification of families below the poverty line lies with the State government. Though the Centre has asked the States to set up vigilance committees at the Panchayat level to supervise identification, the success of the scheme will largely depend on how sincere are the agencies entrusted with the responsibility, other things remaining the same.

In order to achieve the seven minimum basic services in particular and the rural development schemes in general, the Centre has instructed the States to constitute vigilance and monitoring committees at the block, district and State levels for the effective implementation of rural development programmes across the country. The government has taken action to strengthen the District Rural Development Agencies (DRDAs) with adequate technical staff at various levels. These are important agencies for poverty alleviation programmes. Thus, at every level of plan efforts, success will depend chiefly on the States' implementation level.

The Common Minimum Programme (CMP) provides a clear indication of the Government's commitment to accelerate the process of economic reforms and to address some areas of weakness that have emerged.

Among the major themes of the CMP are:

— An overarching commitment to growth with social justice.

— A growth target of 7 per cent year in the next 10 years.

— A commitment to fiscal prudence with the goal of reducing the fiscal deficit to below 4% of GDP.

— A commitment to strengthen anti-poverty programmes and target subsidies in favour of the poor.

— A commitment to increase investment in the social sectors.

— A commitment to continue the process of tax reform and bring about a phased reduction in customs duties.

— A commitment to decontroal and reform in the agricultural sector.

— A target of maintaining 12 per cent annual growth of industry.

— A target of $ 10 billion a year of foreign direct investment.

— A commitment to reform and restructuring public sector enterprises, including through disinvestment.

— A commitment to developing the infrastructure sectors through all modes of investment, public and private domestic and foreign.

The Government has moved swiftly to implement the agenda outlined in the CMP.

The programme of tax reform has been carried forward along the lines articulated by the Tax Reforms Commitee, import duties have been reduced for a wide range of products. The intension is to eventually move to duty rates comparable to those prevailing in other developing South-East Asian economies, the Modvat system of rebates of excise tax on imputs to the singly most important industrial sector in India, namely, textiles, has been extended, the surcharge on corporate taxation reduced by half and introduced Minimum Alternate Tax as a measure of broadening the base of taxation.

The Government is committed to fiscal prudence by reducing the fiscal deficit to 5 per cent of GDP for 1996-97 as compared to 5.9 per cent in 1995-96 (Revised Estimates). A number of initiatives to deal with three critical areas of weakness in the economy are: agriculture, infrastructure and social sectors.

In agriculture, the budget has made allocations for strengthening the capital base of the National Bank for Agricultural and Rural Development, the principal refinance institution in agricultural credit. It has also provided funds for re-capitalising Regional Rural Banks and has launched an important new initiative for private local area banks. Agricultural infrastructure will be strengthened through a large special allocation to finance completion of a number of irrigation schemes.

For infrastructure, a number of fiscal incentives are being provided in the budget. The tax holiday earlier provided for power, telecommunications and road transport has been extended to other infrastructure sectors such as water supply, sewerage and irrigation. It also exempts from income-tax the income of dedicated infrastructure funds which invest in equity and debt instruments of infrastructure companies. The existing income tax incentive available for long-term savings under Section 88 of the Income Tax Act has beden extened to include bonds issued by infrastructure companies or by financial institutions leading to infrastructure projects. The budget has also announced the formation of a new Infrastructure Development Finance Company (IDFC) which will fill some critical gaps in financing of commercially viable infrastructure projects. This institution could act as a direct lender, as a refinance institution, as a channel for multilateral funds and as a provider of various types of financial guarantees for infrastructure projects. The intention is that the IDFC will induce investors in India and abroad to make available long-term funds at the lowest market rates. The budget has alo provided resources for the National Highway Authority of India to help fund its operations.

In the social sectors, a number of schemes have been launched to strengthen the provision of basic minimum services and has generally expanded allocations for social services and anti-poverty programmes.

The Government welcomes foreign investment and has taken a number of concrete steps to achieve this objective. The Foreign Investment Promotion Board has been restructured to make the process of foreign investment approval speedier and more transparent. 350 foreign investment projects have been cleared involving a total foreign equity of US $ 4 billion. A new Foreign investment Promotion Council has been established aimed at reaching out to foreign investors and represent their concerns to the Government. The Government has announced that the list of 35 industries which are eligible for automatic approval of foreign investment upto 51 per cent of equity will be expanded in order to accelerate the approval process. The regulations governing foreign institutional investor have been amended to allow these investors to make equity investments in unlisted companies. Hitherto, they were limited to investing in listed companies only. The limit of investment of 5 per cent of total equity in a single company by an individual FII has been rasied to 10 per cent. The Securities and Exchange Board of India (SEBI) regulations are being amended to allow FIIs to set up 100 per cent debt funds to facilitate FII investment in corporate debt instruments. The guidelines for Euro issues have been liberalised to ease access of Indian companies to international capital markets.

In the area of capital markets, landmark legislation enabling the establishment of depositories for share trading has been passed during the Budget session of Parliament. The first depository is expected to become operational in November this year. Stronger guidelines have been issued for disclosure in the offer documents of primary issues and a number of other steps have been taken to strengthen investor protection. New guidelines have been brought out for mutual funds in general and for money market mutual funds in particular.

The process of financial sector reform has been continued on several fronts. Reserve requirements of banks have been reduced; many more public sector banks have reached capital adequacy norms set out several years ago; regulation of interest rates on bank deposits has been reduced so that they remain only on maturities upto one year; and more private sector banks have become operational. Interest rates charged on loans have been comletely deregulated for Regional Rural Banks to improve their financial viability. It has been decided to allow private sector local area banks to be set up which will operate in two or three districts. These banks will be subject to RBI regulations but will have lower initial capital requirements and will benefit from the interest rate deregulation extended to Regional Rural banks. The process of reforms in the banking sector has borne fruit in the form of significant reduction in non-performing asset of public sector banks and higher profits.

Non-Bank Financial Companies (NBFCs) which comply with the dual requirement of credit rating and prudential norms have been allowed freedom to fixed interest rates on deposits. At the same time, the reserve bank of India has imposed a ceiling on interest rates which can be offered by the mutual benefit financial companies (MBFCs) which do not meet the prudential standards set by RBI.

A number of steps have been taken to strengthen the market for Government securities including the issue of guidelines for primary dealers in Government securities. The first set of such dealers have begun operation. Following the announcement in the budget, legislation is being proposed to provide statutory backing to new, Insurance Regulatory Authority. Similarly, quick action has been taken to establish the Disinvestment Commission announced in the budget.

Public sector

Since Independence, the public sector in India has been guided by the Industrial Policy Resolution of 1956, which had as its objectives the acceleration of the rate of economic growth and speeding up of the industrialisation as means of achieving the socialistic pattern of society. Since in the initial phase of industrialisation, the capital was scare, the state sector assumed the predominance and direct responsibility for industrial development. The size of public sector in India is indeed very large. It includes government departments and its compaines whether in the Central or state sector, irrigation and power projects, railways, posts and telegraphs, ordnance factories and other departmental undertakings, banking, insurance, financial and other services. The focus here is however, on the Central public sector enterprises established as Government companies or statutory corporations excluding banking units.

After the initial exuberance of public sector entering into new areas of industrial manufacturing, providing technical services, trading, financial and services sectors, the public enterprises started facing various problems, some of these problems were due to historical reasons, while others were related to poor project management, over-manning, obsolete technology, poor order book positions etc. All these put together, the public sector as a whole started showing results far below the desired level in comparison to the investments made in them.

The Government announced a new Industrial Policy on 24 July 1991 which envisages liberalisation, competitive environment. The new Policy has laid down certain specific areas in respect of the public enterprises which are to be emphasized in order to make them better performers and more competitive. The slient features of the new Industrial Policy on the Public Sector are: (i) Portfolio of public sector investments will be reviewed with a veiw to focus the public sector on strategic, high-tech and essential infrastructure. Whereas some reservation for the public sector is being retained, there would be no bar for area exclusively to be opened up to the private sector selectively. Similarly, the public sector will also be allowed entry in areas not reserved for it; (ii) Public enterprises which are chronically sick and which are unlikely to be turned around will for the formulation of revival, rehabilitation schemes, be referred to the Board for Industrial and Financial Reconstruction (BIFR), or other similar high level institutions created for the purpose. A social security mechanism will be created to protect the interest of workers likely to be affected by such rehabilitation packages; (iii) in order to raise resources and encourage wider public participation, a part of the governement's share-holding in the public sector would be offered to mutual funds, financial institutions, general public and workers; (iv) Boards of public sector companies would be made more professional and given greater powers; (v) there will be a greater thrust on performance improvement through the Memoranda of Understanding (MOU) system through which management would be granted greater autonomy and will be held accountable. Technical expertise on the part of the Goernment would be upgraded to make the MOU negotiations and implementation more effective;

and (vi) to facilitate a fuller discussion on performance, the MOU singed between Government and the public enterprise would be placed in Parliament. While focussing on major management issues, this would also help place matters on day to day operations of public enterprises in their perspective.

As a major step for implementation of the Policy, the Government of India has disinvested varying percentage of its share-holdings in some PSUs. So far, the shares of 39 PSUs, have been disinvested in favour of the financial institutions, mutual funds, banks, foreign institutional investors and the public. This resulted in disinvestment of 152.07 crore share in 39 public sector undertakings and a sum of Rs. 9,794 crore was realised. The shares of these companies are now listed on the stock exchanges. The valuation of the equity of these enterprises on the stock exchanges reflects the preceptions of the public in general and investors in particular of the performance and the expectations of the public from these enterprises. Besides, the Government has also offered a part of its equity holdings in some of these enterprises in favour of the employees, in order to encourage the employees participation in the managements a sence of commitment and belonging to an enterprise.

Over a period of time, the public enterprises have been faced with the chronical sickness and mounting losses. In the case of some of the enterprises, which have incurred huge losses and had eroded their networth, in order to formulate the revival/rehabilitation packages, a number of these enterprises have been referred to the Board for Industrial and Financial Reconstruction (BIFR). So far, 54 sick enterprises have been referred to BIFR for revival/rehabilitation. BIFR makes an independent assessment of the viability or otherwise of a particular enterprise afte keeping in the view points of the owner

(Government), the employees, the financial institutions and the other concerned. Under the new Industrial Policy, greater thrust has been laid on the evaluation of the performance, through the system of MOUs which has also started yielding positive results in the form of better performance from the public enterprises.

There has been appreciable growth in the investments in the public sector over the years. In 1951, the investment in five Central Public Sector was Rs. 29 crore. This investment has gone up to Rs. 147,587 crore in 245 enterprises as on 31 March 1993 and at Rs. 164,332 crore in 246 enterprises in 1993-94. Thus, during 1993-94, the investment in public sector has increased by Rs. 16,745 crore registering an increase of 11.35 per cent. The overall financial performance of the manufacturing and service group enterprises for the last two years is satisfactory.

Corporate sector

First company legislation in India was an Act for registration of joint stock companies enacted in 1850. This was followed by the Companies Act, 1913. As a result of recommendations of a committee under the chairmanship of C.H. Bhabha to make suggestions for company law reform, the Companies Act, 1956 was enacted as a Central lefislation. Prior to enactment of this Act, administration of companies' legislation was the responsibility of the state governments.

The Companies Act, 1956 has been in force for the last 38 years and during this period it has been amended over 16 times. Amendments of 1969, 1974, 1977 and 1988 are of special importance. By the amendment Act of 1969, system of appointing managing agencies or secretaries or treasurers in companies was abolished. Under the 1974 amendment, powers of High Court relating to certain sections of the Companies Act were transferred to

Company Law Board. Scope of Section 43A was enlarged so as to treat large private limited companies as deemed public limited companies. A new Section 58A was inserted to regulate acceptance of deposits by companies. Section 108A to Section 108H were introduced to check take-over bids by large groups. The 1977 amendment inserted, inter alia Section 634A enabling Company Law Board to enforce its orders under Section 17, 18, 19, 79 141 and 186 of the Act as a decree of a court of law. The Companies Act, 1956 provides various powers to Central Government and Company Law Board, to monitor, regulate and control the affairs of companies. Salient features of the 1988 amendments are: (a) setting up of an independent Company Law Board to exercise such judicial and quasi-judicial functions as are presently being exercised either by Court or Central government and proposed to be transferred to that Board; (b) dispensing with Government approval for managerial appointments and remuneration, subject to fulfilment of certain statutory guidelines which are proposed to be incorporated in the Act itself; (c) delinking of rates of depreciation from rates specified under the Income Tax Act and laying down rates of depreciation in the Act itself to reflect true and fair view of the state of affairs of the company; (d) protecting the interest of investors by providing for intervention by Company Law Board against non-payment of public deposits and certain other matters, compulsory redemption of preference shares in certain cases, requiring companies to disclose reasons for refusal to register transfer of shares, protecting the rights of thee transfree pending mutation of his name in the register of members, and also compulsory lilsting of all public issues; (e) reducing unnecessary cost or burden by requiring companies to attach only an abridged version for disclosure of information relating to conservation of energy, technology absorption, foreign exchange earnings and outgo as well as particulars of employees having some minimum stake in the company and drawing remuneration in excess of that drawn by managerial personnel.

The number of joint stock companies, both Government and non-Government incorporated under the Companies Act, 1956 and at work in India as on 31 March 1994 was 3,08,324. Of these 3,05,625 were limited by shares, 349 with unlimited liability and 2,350 were limited by guarantee or were associations not for profit. The 3,05,625 companies limited by shares have paid up capital of Rs. 1,04,890.8 crore. These comprised 38,000 public limited companies and 2,67,625 private limited companies with paid up capital of Rs. 70,112.1 and Rs. 34,778.7 crore respectively.

During 1993-94, 30,393 companies were registered under the Companies Act. These include 18 Government companies and 30,273 non-government companies with liability limited by shares, 13 non-government companies with unlimited liability and 89 non-government companies with liability limited by guarantee and associations not for profit. Of the 30,291 companies limited by shares registered during the year, 3,625 were public limited companies with an aggregate authorised capital of Rs. 5,456.2 crore and 26,666 were private limited companies with an aggregate authorised capital of Rs. 3,152.1 crore.

Section 60 of the Companies Act requires that prospectuses issued by or on behalf of the companies or in relation to an intended company inviting offers from the public for the subscription or purchase of any shares or debentures be delivered to the Registrar of Companies for registration. Section 67(3) provides that if the offer or invitation can properly be regarded as not being calculated to result, directly or indirectly, in the shares or debentures becoming available for subscription or purchase by persons other than those receiving offer or inviation, as being of a domestic concern of the persons making or receivinng such offer or invitation, shall not be treated as made to the public. Thus, prospectuses for issue of shares or debentures by private placement are not required to be registered with the Registrar of Companies. During the year ending 31 March 1994, 525 non government, non-financial public limited companies delivered to the Registrar of Companies for registration, the copies of prospectuses under Section 60 of the Act raising an amount of Rs. 7,952.8 crore from public as against 426 prospectuses delivered by the companies in the previous year for raising an amount of Rs. 6,331.1 crore. Of the 525 companies which issued prospectuses during 1993-94, 494 companies (or 94 per cent) invited applications for equity share capital, of the remaining 31 companies, invited applications for equity shares as well as debentures and 27 for debentures only.

Of the total amount of Rs. 7,952.8 crore issued through prospectuses during 1993-94, Rs. 3,542.7 crore (44.5 per cent approximately) was in respect of equity shares, Rs. 4,386.1 crore (55.1 per cent approximately) for debentures and balance of Rs. 24 crore (0.3 per cent) in respect of preference shares capital amounting to Rs. 4,310.7 crore or 54.2 per cent of the total amount covered by the prsopectuses, was offered to the public and balance of Rs. 3,642.1 crore or 45.8 per cent was earmarked for firm allotment to the promoters, directors, existing shareholders and employees of the companies, non-resident Indians, financial institutions, banks and the state industrial development corporations.

During 1993-94, 259 companies went into liquidation or otherwise became defunct or ceased to work and were struck off under Section 560 (5) of the Companies Act, 1956.

The following five committees of the National Development Council were constituted to go into some of the critical areas of development: (i) Committee on Austerity, (ii) Committee on Population, (iii) Committee on Employment, (iv) Committee on Micro-Level Planning; and (v) Committee on Literacy.

The meeting of the National Development Council held on 5 April 1993 considered the report of the NDC Committee on Austerity. The Council generally endorsed the recommendations of the report of the Committee. It was also decided to set up a NDC Committee on Power. Accordingly, NDC Committee on Power under the Chairmanship of Chief Minister, Maharashtra, was constituted to examine measures to make state electricity boards economically viable by recasting tariffs, improving efficiency and considering delinking of distribution from generation.

A Committee headed by Deputy Chairman, Planning Commission was constituted to evolve a suitable formula for distribution of Central assistance to Non-special Category States. The suggestions made by the Committee were discussed by the NDC in its meeting on 23-24 December 1991, wherein a consensus emerged and a revised formula evolved which was made the basis for allocation of Central Plan assistance to the states for the Eighth Plan. Under the criterion of the progress in respect of national objectives, the approved formula highlights four objectives, viz., (a) population control and maternal and child health; (b) universalisation of primary education; (c) on-time completion of externally aided projects; and (d) land reforms.

During the 43 year period (1950-51 to 1993-94), Net National Product (NNP) at factor cost at 1980-81 prices increased from 40,454 crore to Rs. 2,02,670 crore implying compound growth rate of 3.8 per cent per annum.

Advance estimates of GDP for 1994-95 project a growth rate of 5.3 per cent over 1993-94.

During the First Five year Plan (1951-56), national income increased by 3.6 per annum. In the Second Five Year Plan (1956-61), however, the growth rate actually achieved was four per cent annum against the target of 4.5 per cent per annum.

In the Third Plan (1961-66), there was a sharp decline in the growth rate at 2.3 per cent per annum and fell well short of the target at 5.6 per cent per annum. This was primarily due to the steep fall in agricultural production and consequent decline in NNP at factor cost of 4.65 per cent in the last year of the Third Plan. However, during the subsequent three Annual Plans, the economy picked up and the growth rate during 1965-69 was 3.7 per cent per annum. Fourth Five year Plan (1969-74), the growth rate target was fixed at 5.7 per cent in terms of NDP at factor cost. However, the actual growth rate achieved was only 3.3 per cent per annum.

The economy took an up-turn during the Fifth Five Year Plan (1974-79). The growth rate fixed in terms of GDP at factor cost of 4.4 per cent per annum was over-achieved at 4.8 per cent annum for the Fifth Five Year Plan. In 1979-80, however, the economy faced a severe drought resulting in the decline of GDP at factor cost by 5.2 per cent over the previous year. The economy bounced back on the track during the Sixth Plan (1980-85) period when the rate of growth in GDP at factor cost at 5.6 per cent per annum surpassed the target of 5.2 per cent per annum. Despite successive drought condistions during the first three years of the Seventh Plan (1985-90), the economy has fared exceptionally well. The growth rate achieved during Deventh Plan period was six per cent per annum and this surpassed the target of five per cent per annum in GDP at factor cost for the Seventh Plan.

During 1991-92, the country faced a severe fiscal crisis and the balance of payment situation became so critical that exceptional measures had to be restored to. While the growth momentum enabled an increase in GDP by 5.4 per cent in 1990-91, the growth in 1991-92 was only 0.9 per cent. In 1992-93 the economy registered the growth of 4.3 per cent and this had been mainly due to high growth in agriculture and improvement in sectors of trade, hotel and restaurants, transport by other means, storage, communication and the public administration and defence, despite railways and banking and insurance sectors registering a decelerated growth. The GDP from agriculture and allied sectors recorded a growth of 5.1 per cent in 1992-93 as compared to 2.3 per cent in 1991-92.

Important policy reforms had been made during June 1991 towards liberalisation and structural adjustment of the economy. These measures have started showing results. The annual rate of inflation as measured by the wholesale price index declined from 13.6 per cent at the end of 1991-92 to seven per cent in 1992-93. The inflation rate stood at 10.8 per cent in 1993-94. The Eighth Plan has targeted for a GDP growth of 5.6 per cent per year, a substantial reduction in the average annual inflation rate, about five per cent and the average current account deficit of about 1.6 per cent of GDP.

Index of agricultural production with the triennium ending 1969-70 as base, rose from 71.9 at the end of First Plan to 86.7 at the end of Second Plan. During Third Plan performance of agriculture was not quite satisfactory. Widespread drought during 1965-67 slowed down the rate of growth in agricultural production and led to increased import of foodgrains and other items. Index of agricultural production reached the level of 80.8 in 1965-66 and 80.7 in 1966-67. These drought years also witnessed introduction of the best available agricultural technology for the first time in India in the form of high yield variety programme and multiple cropping programme. The folloeing years recorded substantial improvement in agricultural production. As a result, the index, after recovering to 98.9 points in 1967-68 increased steadily to 112.4 in 1973-74. The next year 1974-75 again a bad year for agriculture when the index declined to 108.6. This was followed by considerable improvement in 1975-76 when it touched 125.1. In 1976-77, the index registered a decline of 8.8 points and stood at 116.3 but again shot up to 132.9 in 1977-78 and 138 in 1978-79. The year 1979-80 witnessed a fall by 21 points when index number of agricultural production slipped to 117. It recovered to 135.3 in 1980-81.

The index number of agriculture production steadily rose to 158.4 in 1985-86. There was decline during 1986-87 to 152.5 and 151.3 in 1987-88. Thereafter it picked up steadily to 192 in 1990-91 and came down to 188.5 in 1991-92 and recovered to 195.8 in 1992-93. According to the revised triennium ending 1981-82 as base, the index numbers of agriculture production which stood at 85.9 in 1970-71 rose to 154.8 in 1993-94. During 1982-83 Kharif production was adversely affected due to wayward monsoon which was inadequate, uneven and untimely. Even so, fall in foodgrains production was only marginal, indicated by a drop of 5.4 points in the production index. Agricultural production registered significant improvement in 1983-84 which was near normal year from the point of view of weather conditions. Index of agricultural production increased from 137.5 in 1982-83 to 156.4 in 1983-84 and production of foodgrains touched a record level of 15,237 crore tonnes. Weather conditions during 1984-85 were not very satisfactory. As a result, production of foodgrains declined to 14,554 crore tonnes and index number of agricultural production also declined marginally to 154.6. During Kharif 1985, onset of the south-west monsoon was delayed over central and northern states and its behaviour during the season was erratic over many states. However, weather conditions during the rabi season were on the whole rather favourable to crop production. Consequently, foodgrains output during 1985-86 stood at 15.044 crore tonnes. Weather conditions during 1986-87 continued to be unsatisfactory. Monsoon was delayed over eastern states, while southern states experienced dry spells leading to moisture stress conditions. As a result only 14.342 crore tonnes of foodgrains production could be achieved during 1986-87. The year 1987-88 witnessed severe drought conditions in most parts of the country and the incidence of heavy floods in the eastern states. The foodgrains production consequently further fell down to 14.035 crore tonnes. During 1988-89 production of foodgrains recorded a new peak of 16,982 crore tonnes indicating a substaintial increase of 1.775 crore tonnes over the previous peak of 15.237 crore tonnes achieved in 1983-84. With the rainfall and weather situation being favourable during south-west monsoon 1989, the total foodgrains production reached another record level of 17.065 crore tonnes.

On account of erratic behaviour of south-west monsoon, foodgrains production in 1991-92 fell by 4.6 per cent to 16.337 crore tonnes from a record level of 17.64 crore tonnes in 1990-91. Production of rice and wheat was 7.467 crore tonnes and 5.676 crore tonnes respectively. There was a substantial decline in the production of coarse cereals and pulses. Production of oilseeds in 1991-92 was less than previous year's production of 18.60 crore tonnes. Production of foodgrains during 1992-93 was 17.948 crore tonnes and the production was recorded at 18.212 crore tonnes in 1993-94. Production of foodgrains during 1994-95 is expected to be of the order of 18.636 crore tonnes.

Production of oilseeds is expected to be around 2.251 crore tonnes. The thrust has been given for the growth and diversification of agriculture to achieve self-sufficiency in food and generate surpluses for exports during the Eighth Five year Plan Period (1992-97).

On the irrigation side the potential created on major, medium and minor schemes increased from 22.6 million ha in 1950-51 to 26.25 million ha at the end of the First Plan, 29.08 million ha by Second Plan, 33.57 million ha at the end of Third Plan 37.1 million ha by 1966-69. At the end of 1969-74 the potential created was 44.10 ha. By 1979-80, it touched 56.61 million ha and by 1984-85, it reached 65.22 million ha. Potential created by 1989-90 was 76.52 million ha by 1991-92, 81.09 million ha and by 1992-93 achievement was 83.01 million ha. The anticipated achievement by 1993-94 is 85.05 million ha. The target for 1994-95 isto create additional irrigation potential of 2.62 million hectare.

Under power sector, total installed capacity (including non-utility), which was only 2301 mw in 1950, increased to 78,367 mw by the end of March 1992. Against the capacity addition of 30,538.7 mw in public utilities envisaged during the Eighth Plan period (1992-97), the actual addition during the first three years (1992-95) were 12,674 mw.

Under the rural electrification programme, 4.70 lakh villages had been electrified out of 5.79 lakh villages (as per 1981 Census) by the end of the Seventh Plan, achieving 81.3 per cent level of electrification. Upto December 1994, 4.94 lakh villages were electrified.

Universal elementary education, eradication of illiteracy in the age group of 15-35 and development of vocational education to act as viable alternate stream have been the focal points of all programmes in the education sector during the Eighth Plan. Major initiatives in the form of Operation Black-board, non-formal education programme, Teacher Education, and District Primary Education Programme have been undertaken to achieve the goal of 'Education for All'. As on September 1993, 108.20 million children have been enrolled in primary schools and 39.91 million in upper primary schools. The Eighth Plan during its first three years could achieve an additional enrolment of 11.69 million in the primary schools and 7.06 million in upper primary sections making a total enrolment of 18.7 million during the Eighth Plan.

The emphasis of adult literacy programme has been on sustainability of literacy skills and the achievement of goals of rmediation, continuation and application of skills of actual living conditions. Total Literacy Campaign (TLC) and Post Literacy and continuing education programmes are designed to cater to the above objectives. The Eighth Plan target was to cover 100 million adult illiterates by 1991. About 41 million people have been made literate so far under various programmes.

Under Vocational Education, the Eighth Plan target is to divert about 11.63 lakh higher secondary students to the vocational stream. Upto the end of 1993-94, 9.12 lakh students were enrolled in 16,450 vocational sections approved in 570 schools. In order to boost the programme and activities in Vocational Education, Pt. Sunder Lal Sharma Central Institute of Vocational Education (PSSCIVE) has been established under NCERT at Bhopal on 1 July 1993.

In the higher education sector as on 1994, there are 153 universities, 34 demand universities, 7,958 colleges and total enrolment in the higher education system is about 48 lakh. In addition, there ia a vast network for technical education, including colleges and institutions offering courses in engineering, medical science, management, etc. In the technical education sector new initiatives like Technology Development Missions, establishemnt off corpus fund in the case of IITs, IIMs and IISc, Banglaore have been taken up recently.

Large investments in the industrial and mineral sector particularly from the beginning of the Second Plan have brought about a significant transformation in the industrial scene. This rate of industrial growth has not been uniform during this period. After a steady growth of about eight per cent during the initial period of 14 years, there was fluctuating trend in the industrial growth rate approaching near stagnancy in 1960-68, going upto a level of 9.6 per cent in 1976-77 and dropping to -1.6 per cent in 1979-80. During the last decade (1970-71 to 1979-80) the average growth rate has been about four per cent per annum. The average growth rate of industry in the Sixth Plan period (1980-85) amounts to nearly six per cent which is a small improvement over the average of about 5.3 per cent in the preceding five years.

Seventh Plan envisaged an average annual growth rate of 8.7 per cent in the output of industry sector. In the first year of the Seventh Plan i.e. 1985-86, the actual growth rate achieved was 8.7 per cent as per revised Index of Industrial Production (IIP) (Base 1980-81=100). In 1986-87, second year of the Seventh Plan, growth rate achieved was 9.2 per cent. However in 1987-88, the growth rate declined to 7.3 per cent due to decline in production towards the end of the year following unprecedented drought. In 1988-89, there was agian a recovery in the growth rate and the IIP recorded an increase to 8.7 per cent. In the last year of the Seventh Plan, there was slight deceleration in the growth rate, which was only 8.6 per cent due to sharp decline in growth rates of mining and electricity sectors. During

1990-91, the growth rate was 8.3 per cent and during 1991-92, the growth rate was 0.6 for industrial production. The industrial production registered an increase of 2.3 per cent in 1992-93 and 4.1 per cent in 1993-94.

Government initiated a number of measures late in Sixth Plan and in early years of Seventh Plan with the objective of removing constraints on industrial growth and providing a more liberal and congenial environment for development of industries. A number of steps were taken to liberalise industrial procedures relating to creation of capacity, imports of technology, etc., to encourage competition in Indian industry so as to ensure reasonable prices and improvement in quality. These include re-endorsement of capacities, delicensing of industries including specified MRTP and FERA industries and broad-banding of a large number of industries especially in areas of high technology industries linked with energy production and utilisation, as well as mass consumer goods industries. Provisions of the MRTP Act and FERA regulations were rationalised to facilitate entry into industrial areas of high priority. Expansion of existing units has been liberalised and investment in moderanisation/renovation/replacement as well as export production, has been exempted from industrial licensing. Licensing of new capacity has been liberalised and concept of minimum economic scale introduced to promote production efficiency, taking advantage of economics of scale.

A number of policy measures have been initiated for development of specific industries like textiles, sugar, steel, electronics, etc. Steps have also been taken to tackle the problem of industrial sickness. These include (i) system for early detection of industrial sickness introduced by Reserve Bank of India' (ii) various steps for checking industrial sickness and promoting industrial revival evolved by Industrial Reconstruction Bank of India; (iii) setting up of Board for Industrial and Financial rreconstruction, and (iv) setting up of Small Industries Development Fund in IDBI to provide refinancing assistance not only for development, expansion and modernisation but also for rehabilitation of sick industrial units in small scale sector. The statement on industrial policy announced in July 1991 is being implemented. The new industrial policy emphasises delicensing and technological dynamism. Government has also set up modernisation funds for textiles and jute industries to cater to problems of those industries which account for major share of industrial sickness.

The Government is to establish 70 growth centres to act as a nucleus for industrial growth and promote accelerated development especially in backward areas. Sixty nine centres have already been identified. The process of setting up of the growth centres has been started. There has been an important milestone in the public sector steel capactiy with most of the main units of the Stage-I of the Visakhapatnam Steel Plant having come on stream in 1990-91. The 4 MT expansion programmes of Bhillai Steel Plant and Bokaro Steel Plant have also fully materialised during the year.

Technical advice and assistance to small scale manufacturers is provided by the Small Industries Development Organisation through its network of 16 service institutes, 16 branch institutes, 58 extension, production and training centres. The organisation also provides common service and tool room facilities in workshops attached to small industries, service institutes and extension centres. It conducts courses in management and technical disciplines. During 1974-75, it provided technical assistance to 1,02,684 entrepreneurs and visited 70,965 factories for spot guidance.

Two new centres namely the Central Insititute of Tool Design, Hyderabad, and The Institute for Design of Electrical Measuring Instruments, Bombay, have started providing technical guidance and training for entrepreneurs.

The National Small Industries Corporation, which was set up in 1955, operates the scheme of procuring machinery for small-scale manufacturers on a hire-purchase basis on concessional terms. The value of machines delivered under this scheme during the period April-October 1974 was Rs. 5.69 crores as against Rs. 3.25 crores during the corresponding period of the previous year. It also assists the small-scale sector in processing orders from government departments and agencies. The value of stores purchased by the Directorate General of Supply and Disposals from April to November 1974 was about Rs. 37 crores. The Prototype Development and Training Centres set up with American, West German and Japanese assistance at Rajkot, Okhla (Delhi) and Howrah impart training to persons engaged in small-scale industries.

Hitherto the emphasis was minly on agro-based industries. The growth of these industries was no doubt important for providing a ready market to the agricultural outputs, to create employment opportunities in view of seasonal nature of agriculture and to stabilise the farmer's income. Several specialised agencies such as the State Finance Corporations, Small Scale Reserve Bank, and the various technical guidance and assistance schemes of the Central Government, State Governments, Reserve Bank and State Bank of India were directed mainly to sustain the growth of small scale and cottage industries.

It was, however, realised at a later stage that the institutional at the "output" end is only one part of the game. Indian agriculture does not face any serious problem from the demand side. It is with the improvement in the technique of production that the cost of farming can be reduced and the productivity of the land can be improved in order to meet ever growing demandof agricultural outpout from direct consumers as well as from industries. The institutional set-up was, therefore, geared up to discover means for improving the technique of agricultural production and also to manufacture agriculture machinery.

At the highest level various agricultural research centres, headed by Indian Council of Agriculture Research, are performing important functions in the development and distribution of scientific knowledge of agriculture. There is also the Indian Society of Agriculture Engineers which provides a wealth of information for the application of science and technology to farming. At the village level cooperative societies are propagating and, where possible, implementing, the programmes of the research centres.

Cooperative societies and various official organisations have performed important functions but because of their limitations, these agencies could not meet the requirements of mechanised agriculture which has recetly gained importance for improving agricultural productivity.

Thus woith a view to meeting the rapidly growing demand of farmers for standard agricultural machinery equipment, e.g., tractors, power tillers, power threshers, seed-cum-fertilisers, drills, power sprayers and dusters, diesel and electric pump-sets, on cash or hire-purchase basis, the State Agro-Industrial Corporations have been established by the Government.

These corporations have been established in almost all the states. They are performing multifarious activities connected with not only the supply of agricultural machinery but also providing credit for the purpose. Some of them have ambitious programmes of designing and assembling tractors and manufacturing various tools and implements. But in fairness to the Corporations it must be recorded that none of them is more than three years old. What is more, some of them have the right ideas. In Gujarat, for instance, the AIC has decided to accord priority to the setting up of new cold storage plants in Banaskantha and Balsar, onion dehydration plants at Jamnagar and Bhavnagar and hydrogenated oil unit in the Saurashtra region. In West Bengal, the AIC will supply diesel pumping sets to poor farmers owning two to five acres of land on payment of Rs. 70 cash down, the balance of the price–Rs. 3,500–being recoverable in easy instanlments. In Tamil Nadu the AIC is not only going into the processing and marketing of farm produce but will also set up factories for the servicing and repair of the 1,000 new tractors which are sold in the state every year.

It is evidnt that the growth of agro-industries cannot reverse the process of urbanisation. Most of the plants for processing farm products or "waste" materials released by the existing agro-based industries like textiles must bc established near the consuming centres if they are to pave their way. All that can be done in the circumstances is to establish new industrial units, both big and small, in district towns and away from the major cities. Any effort to confine the new agro-industries to the rural or semi-urban areas is bound to hinder their growth and will in the end be self-defeating.

Since there are quite a number of common problems which these institutions are likely to face, it might be worthwhile to establish a Central Agro-Industrial Corporation of India to coordinate the work of these state institutions. Besides coordinating the working of the state corporations, the central organisation can be entrusted with research and development of technology. Centralisation of research will eliminate waste and duplication. The State Corporations will, however, continue to collect data rom their regional offices to make them available to the central organisation. It will also be the task of the cental agency to arrange the production of different components of machinery and implements in different areas according to the local facilities available on the "comparative cost" basis. The proposed corporation can also serve as an effective agency in arranging the colllection of technical knowledge from abroad and distribution of imported machinery.

The massive expenditure that the Government has incurred on agricultural development has in one way or another gone to prop up a new rich class by passing millions of small farmers and landless labourers. There are growing indications of discontent among those who have found the cost of acquiring modern equipment and agricultural inputs soaring, on the one hand, and official and somehow getting channelled away from them, on the other.

The Government's decision to establish 500 pilot agro-service centres in the country is a step in the right direction. The programme is being jointly sponsored by the Ministry of Agriculture and the Ministry of Industrial Development and is designed to provide a wide range of services from custom-hiring of tractors and other farm equiptment and repair and maintenance of agricultural machinery to soil testing, crop spraying, water anaylsis and land and field services such as levelling and contour surveying. The scheme is intended to provide employment in the rural area as well as to accelerate the process of modernisation in the villages. It is particularly aimed at providing help to the small farmers and the weaker sections of the rural community in the relatively backward areas. The rapid increase in the use of tractors, pumps, mechanical threshers and other machines, not to speak of community radios, transistors and other personal gadgetry, has created a demand for easily available repair and maintenance facilities on a wide scale. Then agro-service centres can perform a valuable function provided they are suitably staffed and have the requisite managerial competence. The Government has negotiated World Bank assistance for tractor-cum-groundwater development projects in Punjab, Haryana and Tamil Nadu. Agro-service centres could be established alongside these programmes for a start.

As far as mechanical equipment like tractors and pumps are concerned, it would be most' desirable for the country to standardise on a few broad categories (not necessarily makes) so that problems of maintenance and the stocking of parts and components are not needlessly complicated by type differences. Little thought appears to have been given to this matter so far. But it is obviously something that calls for an early policy consideration.

Revenue

Direct taxes play a significant role in the tax system not only as a revenue source but as a powerful instrument for achieving social and economic objectives. Firstly, direct taxes help make tax systemprogressive and reduce disparities in distribution of income and wealth. Secondly, they subserve the strategy of planning in many ways. Differential taxation of savings in specified assets helps promote savings and induce flow of investment into desirable channels. In India, both income tax as well as taxes on capital, are designed to serve these objectives. The Income Tax Department administers a number of direct taxes Acts, namely, the Income Tax Act, 1953 (discontinued in respect of death on or after 16 March 1985); the Companies (Profit) Surtax Act, 1964 (discontinued from 1 April 1988); The Hotel Receipts Tax Act, 1987.

The Budget presented in 1995 has sought to accelerate the pace of reforms and modernisation of the Indian direct tax system that began three years ago. Some of the Important steps taken in that direction include tax incentives to boost up infrastructure development, expansion of the tax base by enlarging the scope of withholding of taxes, for the rationalisation of the tax structure and measures to combat black money by introduction of special procedure for speedy assessment in search cases.

The Income Tax Department is continously taking necessary legislative and administrative steps from time to time to curb/control black money and is also striving to check tax evasion and accumulation of unaccounted wealth. In pursuance of this objective, systematic surveys, search and seizure operations, verification of information by Central Information Branches in a planned manner and scrutiny of selected cases are undertaken. Persons found to be indulging in tax evasion are dealt with severely by inposing penalties and by launching prosecution proceedings against them.

Customs and Central exercise are the two important sources of the Central Government tax revenue. Revenue collection from Union Excise Duties (excluding cesses administered by other departments) upto December 1994 was Rs. 26,333.62 crore (provisional). While the revenue from Customs duties at the same time was Rs. 18,694.20 crore (provisional). The major policy steps taken towards simplication of excise taxation in 1994-95 ; budget were: (a) The reduction in the number of ad valorem rates to about half the existing number for simplicity and transparency; (b) Reduction in the dispersal of rates in each Chapter of Tariff; (c) Reduction in the number of exemption notifications to about half; (d) Shift in the bulk of excise taxation from secific to ad valorem rates to ensure built in buoyancy of revenues; (e) Continuing the process of lowering rates when they are unduly high; (f) Removal of complicated price list procedure; (g) Extension of modvat to capital goods, petroleum goods and spun yarns. The exercise of the tax reform initiated in Budget 1991-92 was continued in the Budget 1994-95 for simplification of the tax structure and movemnet towards moderate rates of taxation. The main features of customs tariff reform were: (i) The Maximum rate of Customs Duty was reduced to 65 per cent with the exception of passengers baggage, liquor, dried grapes, almonds, ball and roller bearings; (ii) The Customs Duty on Capital goods was further reduced to 25 per cent to boost investment to help domestic capital goods industry; (iii) substantial reduction in the duties on key raw materials, such as steel and chemicals; (iv) Reduction or removal of anomalies caused by important duties on raw materials and components being higher than on finished products; and (v) Elimination of the notification governing the administration of customs duties, thus reducing discretionary power and possibilities for disputes.

India is the largest producer and exporter of opium in the world. Cultivation of poppy and production and export of opium are under exclusive control of the Central Government. Control over opium cultivation have been made stricter inter alia by raising the minimum qualifying yield of opium for grant of licences for the crop year 1994-95 to 43 kg/hectare for the states of Madhya Pradesh, Uttar Pradesh and Rajasthan. A scheme of rewarding the cultivators who tendered higher yields was also intoduced. During 1993-94, India had exported about 619 metric tonnes of opium against production of 416 metric tonnes.

Drive against smugglers, tax evaders and drug traffickers was persued by strengthening of intelligence network and special attention to vulnerable areas. The year 1994-95 has also seen continuing efforts at better coordination with the intelligence and enforcement agences in India and other countries. Post seizure operation like preventive detention, under cofeposa in cases warranting such action, prosecution and adjudication etc., continued to receive special attention.

In addition to tackling of outright smuggling of contraband goods, customs authorities took strict action against certain companies in the organised sector indulging in tax evasion, import frauds, misues of duty exemption scheme, evasion of customs and excise duties and foreign exchange violations. As a result of vigorous anti-smuggling drive during 1994 goods worth Rs. 535.21 crore were seized.

Sales Tax is the most important source of revenue of the states. Levy of taxes on sale or purchase of goods taking place within a state is a state subject. Administration of the Central Sales Tax Act, 1956, under which tax is levied on inter-state sale of goods has been entrusted by law to the state governments who collect and retain the proceeds of such tax. Total collection of Sales Tax covering Central Sales Tax, tax on motor spirit and purchase tax on sugarcane during 1994-95 is estimated at Rs. 32,266.3 crore. Total collection of additional excise duty in lieu of sales tax during 1994-95 on sugar, tobacco and textiles is estimated at Rs. 2,725 crore.

Public debt

Public debt includes internal debt comprising borrowings inside the country like market loans, compensations and other bonds, treasury bills issued to the Reserve Bank of India, state governments, commercial banks and other parties as well as non-negotiable non-interest bearing rupees securities issued to the international financial institutions; and external debt comprising loans from foreign countries, international financial institutions etc. The "other liabilities" include outstanding against the various small saving schemes, provident funds, securities issued to Industrial Development Bank of India, Unit Trust of India and nationalised banks, deposits under the special deposit schemes, reserve funds and deposits.

Banking

Although some form of banking, mainly, money-lending type, has been in existence in India from ancient times, it was only little over a century ago that modern banking took its birth. the earlist institutions which undertook banking business under the British regime were agency houses which carried on banking business, in addition to their trading activities. Most of these agency huses were closed down during 1929-32. A number of banks which came into existence between the thirties and forties of the last century were also in great trouble. Prominent among these were three presidency banks which were later amalgamated into Imperial Bank of India in 1919 following a banking crisis.

The first bank of limited liability managed by Indians was Oudh Commercial Bank founded in 1881. Subsequently the Punjab National Bank was established in 1894. Swadeshi movement which began in 1906 encouraged the formation of a number of commercial banks. Banking crisis in 1913-1917 and failure of 588 banks in various states during the decade ending in 1949, underlined the need for regulating and controlling commercial banks. The Banking Companies (Inspection Ordinance) was passed in January 1946 and the Banking Companies (Restriction of Branches). Act in February 1946. The Banking Companies Act was passed in February 1949 which was subsequently amended to read as Banking Regulation Act. With a view to bringing commercial banks into the mainstream of economic development with definite social obligations and objective, Government issued an Ordinance on 19 July 1969 acquiring ownership and control of 14 major banks in the country, eith deposits exceeding Rs 50 crore each. Six more commercial banks were nationalised from 15 April 1980.

The objectives of public sector banking system were outlined on 21 July 1969. Some of them are to: (a) mobilise savings of people to the largest possible extent and utilise them for productive purposes; (b) operations of banking system should be promoted by a larger social purpose and should be subject to close public regulation; (c) cater to the legitimate credit needs of private sector industry and trade, big or small; (d) ensure that needs of productive sectors of the economy and in particular those of farmers, small scale industrialists and self-employed professional groups are met in an increasing manner; (e) nationalised banks to actively foster the growth of the new and progressive entrepreneurs and create fresh opportunities for hitherto neglected and backward areas in different parts of the country and (f) to curb the use of bank credit for speculative and other unproductive purposes.

Planning

Planning in India derives its objectives and social promises from Directive principles of State Policy enshrined in the Constitution. Public and private sectors are viewed as complementary. Private sector covers not only organised industry but also small scale industries, agriculture, trade and a great deal of activity in housing, construction and other fields. Individual effort and private initiative are considered necessary and desirable in national endeavour on development with optimkum of voluntary cooperation. Although in the past, economic planning did envisage a growing public sector with massive investments in basic and heavy industries, now the emphasis on the public sector is less pronounced and the current thinking on planning in the country, in general, is that it should increasingly be of an indicative nature.

Planning Commission was set up in 1950 to prepare the blue-print of development, taking an overall view of the needs and resources of the country.

The First Plan (1951-56) had a two fold objective to correct the disequilibrium in economy caused by the Second World War and partition of the country and also to initiate simultaneously a process of all-round balanced development. This was ensure increase in the national income and steady improvement in living standards. Keeping in view large-scale imports of foodgrains in 1951 and inflationary pressure on economy, the Plan accorded the highest priority to agriculture including irrigation and power projects. About 44.6 per cent of the total outlay of Rs. 2,069 crore in the public sector (later raised to Rs. 2,378 crore) was allotted for its development. The Plan also aimed at increasing the rate of investment from five to about seven per cent national income.

In 1954, Parliament decleared that the broad objectives of economic policy should be to achieve a 'socialistic pattern of society' under which the basic criteria for determining the lines of advance would be social gaín and greater equality in income and wealth and not private profit. The Second Five Year Plan (1956-57 to 1960-61), therefore, sought to promote a pattern of development which sould ultimatley lead to the establishment of a socialistic pattern of society in India. In particular, it stressed that the benefits of economic development should accrue more to the relatively less privileged sections of society and there should be a progressive reduction in the concentration of incomes, wealth and economic power.

The main aims of the Second Plan were: (i) an increase of 25 per cent in the national income; (ii) rapid industrialisation with particular emphasis on the development of basic and heavy industries; (iii) large expansion of employment opportunities; and (iv) reduction of inequalities in income and wealth and more even distribution of economic power. The Plan also aimed at increasing the rate of investment from about seven per cent of the national income to 11 per cent 1960-61. The Plan laid special stress on industrialisation, increased production of iron and steel, heavy chemicals including nitrogenous fertilizers and development of heavy engineering and machine-building industry.

The Third Plan (1961-62 to 1965-66) aimed at securing a marked advance towards self-sustaining growth. Its immediate objectives were to: (i) secure an increase in the national income of over five per cent annum and at the same time ensure a pattern of investment which could sustain this rate of growth during subsequent Plan periods; (ii) achieve self-sufficiency in foodgrains and increase agricultural production to meet the requirements of industry and exports; (iii) expand basic industries like steel, chemicals, fuel and power and to establish machine-building capacity, so that the requirements of further industrialisation could be met within a period of 10 years or so mainly from the country's own resources; (iv) utilise fully the manpower resources of the country and ensure substantial expansion in employment opportunities; and (v) establish progresively greater equality of opportunity and bring about reduction in disparities of income and wealth and a more even distribution of economic power. The Plan aimed at increasing the national income by about 30 per cent from Rs. 14,500 crore in 1960-61 to about Rs. 19,000 crore by 1965-66 (at 1960-61 prices) and per capita income by about 17 per cent from Rs. 330 to Rs. 385 during the same period.

The situation created by the Indo-Pakistan conflict in 1965, two successive years of severe drought, devaluation of the currency, general rise in prices and erosion of resources available for Plan purposes delayed finalisation of the Fourth Five Year Plan. Instead, between 1966 and 1969, three Annual Plans were formulated within the framework of the draft outline of the Fourth Plan. They took into account the conditions prevailing at that time. The state of the economy and the non-availablity of financial resources for Plan purposes kept down the size of development outlay during this period.

The Fourth Plan (1969-74) aimed at accelerating the tempo of development and reducing fluctuations in agricultural production as well as a the impact of uncertainties of foreign aid. It sought to raise the standard of living through programmes designed to promote equality andsocial justice. The Plan laid particular emphasis on improving condition of less privileged and weaker sections especially through provision of employment and education. Efforts were also directed towards reduction of concentration and wider diffusion of wealth, income and economic power.

The Plan aimed at inincreasing net domestic production at 1968-69 factor cost from Rs. 29,071 crore in 1969-70 to Rs. 38,306 crore in 1973-74. In terms of 1960-61 prices, this implied an increase from Rs. 17,351 crore in 1968-69 to Rs. 22,862 crore in 1973-74. Average annual compound rate of growth envisaged was 5.7 per cent.

The Fifth Plan (1974-79) was formulated against the backdrop of severe inflationary pressures. Major objectives of the Plan were to achieve self-reliance and adopt measures for raising consumption standards of people living below the poverty line. This Plan also gave high priority to bring inflation under control and to achieve stability in the economic situation. It targeted an annual growth rate of 5.5 per cent in national income. Four Annual Plans pertaining to the Fifth Plan period were completed. It was subsequently decided to end the Fifth Plan with the close of Annual Plan 1978-79 and initiate work for a new Plan for next five years with new priorities and programmes.

The Sixth Plan (1980-85) was conceptualised keeping in view achievements and shortcomings of the past three decades of planning. Removal of poverty was foremost objective of the Plan even though it was recognised that task of this magnitude could not be accomplished in a short period of five years. The strategy adopted for the Plan consisted essentially in moving simultaneously towards strengthening infrastructure for both agriculture and industry so as to create conditions for an accelerated growth in investments, output and exports and provide through special programmes designed for the purpose, increased opportunities for employment especially in rural areas and unorganised sector and as well meeting minimum basic needs of people. Stress was laid on dealing with inter-related problems through a system approach rather than in separate cmpartments, greater management efficiency and intensive monitoring in all sectors and active involvement of people in formulating specific schemes of development at local level and securing their speedy and effective implementation.

Sixth Plan's actual expenditure stood at Rs. 1,09,291.7 crore (current prices) as against the envisaged total public sector outlay of Rs. 97,500 crore (1970-80 prices) accounting for a 12 per cent increase in nominal terms. Average annual growth rate for the Plan was 5.2 per cent, targeted growth rate for this period.

The Seventh Plan (1985-90) emphasised on Policies

and programmes, the aim of which had been rapid growth in foodgrains production production, employment opportunities and productivity within the framework of basic tenets of planning, namely, growth, modernisation, self-relience and social justice. Due to overall fovourable weather conditions, implementation of various thrust programmes and with concerted efforts of the government and the farmers, foodgrains production during the Seventh Plan grew by 3.23 per cent as compared to along term growth rate of 2.68 per cent during 1967-68 to 1988-89 and a growth rate of 2.255 per cent in eighties. To reduce unemployment and, consequently, the incidence of poverty, special programmes like Jawahar Rozgar Yojana were initiated in addition to the already existing programmes. Due recognition was also accorded to the role small scale and food-processing industries can play in this regard. Various policy instruments were used to improve the productivity and the international competitiveness of the Indian economy. Instead of creating new facilities, the thrust was on improvement of existing facilities, and fuller capacity utilisation.

The total expenditure during the entire Seventh Plan stood at Rs. 2,18,729.62 crore (current price) as against the envisaged total public sector outlay of Rs. 1,80,000 crore, resulting in a 21.52 per cent increase in nominal terms. During this Plan period, Gross Domestic product (GDP) grew at an average rate of 5.6 per cent per year exceeding the targeted growth rate by 0.6 per cent

The Eight Five Year Plan (1990-95) could not take off due to the fast changing political situation at the Centre. The new government which assumed power at the Centre by June 1991 decided that the Eighth Five Year Plan would commence on 1 April 1992 and that 1990-91 and 1991-92 should be treated as separate Annual Plans. Formulated within the framework of the earlier Approach to the Eighth Five Year Plan (1990-95), the basic thrust of these Annual Plans were on maximisation of employment and social transformation.

The Plan proposes a growth rate of 5.6 per cent per annum on an average during the Plan period. The level of national investment is proposed at Rs. 7,98,000 crore and the public sector outlay of Rs. 4,34,100 crore. Consistent with the expected resource position, the size of the plans of the states and union territories is projected at Rs. 1,86,235 crore and of the Central Plan at Rs. 2,47,865 crore.

The Annual Plan 1992-93 envisaged a total public sector outlay of Rs. 80,771.96 crore, actual expenditure came down to Rs. 72,853 crore which is lower by one per cent than the Budget Estimates for the Plan. The actual size of the Plans for states and union territories was lower by nearly 10 per cent i.e. from Rs. 32,364.88 crore (BE) to Rs. 29,159 crore. The main reasons for the shortfall in State Plans were deterioration in the balance from current revenues, erosion in the contribution of state electricity boards and in some cases of state road transport corporations, negative opening balances,mounting non-plan expenditure, shortfalls in the collection of small savings, etc.

The envisaged total public sector outlay of Rs. 1,00,120.16 crore for the Annual Plan 1993-94 on revision came down to Rs. 92,623.64 crore which is lower by 7.48 per cent that the budget estimates for the Plan. In the Central Sector, the approved outlay was Rs. 61,453.53 crore. The total outlay of the plans for states and union territories on revision was lower by 13.84 per cent i.e. from Rs. 36,184 crore in the budget estimates to Rs. 31,175.11 crore in revised estimates. The main reasons for the shortfall in states plans were deteriorating in the balance from current revenues, erosion in the contribution of state electricity boards and in some cases of state road transport corporations, negative opening balances, mounting non-plan expenditure, shortfall in the collection of small savings, etc.

The Annual Plan 1994-95 provides for a public sector outlay of Rs. 1,12,197 crore at current prices. At 1991-92 prices it would be about 20 per cent of the envisaged Eighth Plan public sector outlay. The state plans outlay is Rs. 39,992 crore at current prices, which works out to 35.64 per cent of public sector outlay and 17.17 per cent of the Eighth Plan provision for the states at 1991-92 prices. In the first three years, assuming that the actual outlays will be the same as the revised estimates of 1993-94 and the budget estimates of 1994-95 will be reallised, the public sector outlays in the Central Plan and the State Plans will work out to 59 per cent and 44 per cent of the respective Eighth Plan provisions, at constant prices.

An era of planning thus started in 1951, when the First Five Year Plan was launched. This was followed by the Second Five Year Plan (1955-56) and the Third Five Year Plan (1960-61). All these developments, from the Grow More Food Campaign in 1942 to the planned economy, are discussed separately. On the whole, the country lacked any well-defined policy of agriculture up to the end of Second Five Year Plan. Many improvements have taken place since then.

Cooperative farming, declared at one stage as the ultimate form of organisation for agricultural production, did not receive wide acceptance and that accounts for lack of any serious effort or enthusiastic response to its implementation. To achieve social justice, ceiling on the size of holdings is being imposed but there is considerable confusion in matters of detail and execution. Adequate investigations are lacking to justify the measure economically. There is good cultivable land which is lying waste in some states not because the ownership rights are vested in persons who are not able to farm it themselves but also because they do not lease it out for fear of losing their title to it. To the extent such land is brought under cultivation, the measure may prove beneficial. But where the holdings are pushed down below a certain minimum size, it is not easy to predict the effect on agricultural efficiency and production.

Quite often the emphasis on increasing the production of foodgrains has led to a fall in the production of commercial crops, leading to shortage of such products. In turn a cry is raised to increase the production of cash crops. Such an action can hardly be called a policy. Not much thought was given to preparing the estimates of cost-benefit ratio in undertaking programmes of large-scale irrigation and land reclamation. Therefore, emhasis has been changing from major to minor irrigation projects and vice versa; similarly from land reclamation to raising the standard and intensity of cultivation on land already under the plough.

These instances make it clear that hardly any well-defined policy existed and much less was pursued. A sound policy calls for precise and detailed information on cost-benefit relationships of various developmental projects, efficiency standards, and farms in various size groups in different farming type regions. First, it is necessary to have a census of agricultural resources, surveys on land use, investigations on factors inhibiting agricultural efficiency regionwise and the demand projections for the current and future needs in respect of food, cash crops, and export. Then taking the country and regions as units, sound plans need to be drawn up for land use, agricultural production, and needed supplies. To support the fulfilment of these targets, ancillary measures need be taken, namely, land reclamation, assistance in raising the intensity of cultivation, credit support, educational programmes, irrigation, etc. All such measures, for successful implementation, need a watchdog in the form of adequate farm management and agricultural economics research to guide and evaluate simultaneously the execution of the programmes in order to make them efficient and effective and to stop those measures which, on experience, have a retrograde effect.

No doubt, steps have been taken towards the direction suggested above, the major lacunae in them may be listed as follows:

— The carrying out of developmental activities on a piecemeal basis with the result that full benefits expected from such programmes have not been obtained. In UP, tube-wells, for example, were dug but could not be commissioned for lack of energisation.

— The budgetary provision for efforts in various directions were made on the basis of administrative divisions and not on a properly estimated requirement of expenditure with the consequence that the efforts were too thinly spread and proved almost futile. The early Grow More Food Campaign is an appropriate example of this.

— The approach where an investment could be most effective from the point of view of natural factors like land, climate or economic factors like demand, particularly in the case of livestock products, has been conspicuous by its absence.

— Duplication and overlapping has often led to futility of efforts which cold never be enough according to needs and urgency.

If we examine any one of the policy measures on prices of foodgrains, production, distribution, land tenure, irrigation, land reclamation and settlement, we will see that each one has some woeful tale to tell. In the functions of the Ministry of Community Development and Cooperation and the Ministry of Agriculture, there was a considerable overlapping till they were recently merged. Between them and even within the same ministry there is duplication of positions. This leads not only to wastage of scarce funds but also to confusion in working.

A number of committees have from time to time gone into the problem of agricultural administration and machinery. All of them have helped to expand agricultural organisation. Mention may be made of the Patel Committee (1945-46) as a result of whose recommendations the Directorate of Economics and Statistics became a separate unit of the Ministry; the enquiry by N. Gopalsawami Ayyanger (1949), which recommended the creation of the Bureau of Natural Resources and Agriculture with a coordinating minister for the Ministries of Agriculture, Food and works; the W.R. Natu Enquiry 1951; and more recently the enquiry Mr. Keifer (1965). Full-scale general enquiries have also been made of the machinery of the Government of India leading to proposals for its reorganisation by Richard Tottenham in 1945, by Shri R.A. Gopalsawami in 1952 and Dr. Appleby in 1954. It may also be mentioned here that the Food Grains Policy Committee, 1947, the Grow More Food Committee 1952 and the Balwantrai Mehta Committee, 1957 also have made recommendations for the reorganisation of the machinery of agricultural administration at different levels. The desire for administrative improvement has been continuous, the suggestions for reform numerous, but the practical results of the enquiries have been rather disappointing.

Piecemeal changes and adjustments have been made from time to time. There has been some bureau shuffling off and on but no thorough reorganisation that could assure the efficient functioning of the machinery for accelerating development.

Agriculture

In order to streamline agricultural production in the country, an Agricultural Board was constituted in 1963. The main function of the Board was to bring about expenditious implementation of the programme for the development of agriculture including animal husbandry, forestry and fisheries. The working of the board was recently reviewed and the Minister of Food, Agriculture, Community Development and Cooperation is its Chairman and the Minister of State in the Ministry of Finance, and the Member Agriculture, Planning Commission, are its members. The function and powers of the board are: (i) to secure effective and continuous coordination between the Centre and the states, in matters relating to the formulation and execution of development programmes; (ii) to review the progress of development programmes, ensure efficient arrangements for supplies and services, locate difficulties, if any, and endeavour to remove them; and (iii) to take such other measures as would ensure speedy and effective implementation of the development programmes at the Centre and in the states. The decisions of the Board will be treated as the decisions of the Government of India as long as they are within the plan provisions and within the framework of the approved budget provisions of the ministries concerned.

The Ministry of Agriculture was reorganised in 1964 on the initiative of the then Minister of Food and Agriculture who had found it a poor instrument for carrying out a dynamic and forward-looking policy aimed at making the country self-sufficient and even surplus in the foodgrains and assuring the prosperity of the farming population. The reorganisation was aimed at making the Ministry "function more effectively and to enable it more actively to associate itself with the implementation of development schemes by the states." It attempted (i) a redistribution of subjects and responsibilities among the various units of the Ministry so as to make the assignments of the units compact and specific; (ii) to assign to scientific and technical officers of the Ministry executive functions and operational responsibilities for planning, implementation and supervision of programmes, in addition to their advisory functions, to secure through "better administrative machinery"; and (iii) closer and more continuous contact between the Central and State Governments in the implementation of agricultural plan schemes and to improve Centre-State relations.

The apex of the structure of administration consists of the Minister of Food and Agriculture, who is a senior member of the Cabinet, and Ministers of State and Deputy Ministers who constitute the political executive. The Secretary of the Ministry is the official head of the Ministry and the principal adviser to the Minister. The Department of Agriculture which is one of the three departments included in the Ministry is organised in eight wings, and has besides five specialised offices, a number of supervisory and operational agencies and some cells and units for certain specific purposes.

The eight wings of the department are: (1) Production; (2) Forestry; (3) Fisheries; (4) Inputs (F) (Fertilisers); (5) Inputs (M) (Machinery); (6) Land problems; (7) Special development programmes; and (8) Coordination. The specialised of offices are: (1) The Indian Council of Agricultural Research; (2) The Directorate General of State Farms; (3) Agricultural Prices

Commission; (4) The Directorate of Extension; and (5) The Directorate of Economics and Statistics.

Lastly, reference may be made to the numerous subordinate and attached offices of the Department which operate various programmes of the Ministry, expert committees and other agencies. The more important attached offices are the Directorate of Plant Protection, the Office of the Agricultural Marketing Advisor, the National Seeds Corporation, the Warehousing Corporation, etc.

Committees, both official and unofficial, expert or representative of interests, have been established to advise the Ministry on many important matters. Fifteen of these have been listed as functioning at present. These are Panel of Economists, Panel of Experts on Agricultural Demonstration and finally Panel of Farmers to advise the Agricultural Prices Commission.

The other agencies falling in this category are: Committee for the Improvement of Agricultural Statistics; National Committee on the Preparation of Farm Management; Manual for the use of Extension Workers; Study Group on Wild Life and Wild Life Products; Indian Board for Wild Life; Central Forestry Commission; Board for Agricultural Machinery and Implements; Standing Committe of Experts on Manures and Fertilisers; National F.A.O. Liaison Committee; Central Council of Gosamvardhana; Central Variety Release Committee; Central Board of Fisheries; and Central Fisheries Research Committee.

The areas covered by these boards and committees are of vital importance to the development of agriculture and it is necessary, therefore, that they should be active bodies manned by competent personnel.

The Planning Commission's role in agricultural administration needs to be examined. It is directly and intimately connected with agricultural development at all stages from policy formulation and planning to plan implementation and evaluation. The Planning Commission's concurrence is required for the ministry's policies and programmes in detail. In fixing the targets of production, in making financial allocations in the five year plan and in the annual plans, in negotiations with the states, the Planning Commission plays a leading, if not dominant role. The working relations between the Planning Commission and the Ministry have not been always smooth and are not infrequently marked by friction.

Multi-Level planning and programme implementation

Apex-planning body at state level is generally state Planning board comprising chief minister as chairman and finance and planning ministers of the state and some technical experts as members. Department of planning in state government provides secretariat for the board. In many states, planning process has been decentralised to district level and in some states even to sub-division or block levels. In most of the states, there is district planning committee or district planning council comprising both official and non-official members. Some states also have a separate set-up consisting of functionaries like district planning officers, economist, credit planners, project appraiser, export training coordinator and an area planner in some of the districts for formulation of district plans, which are integrated with state plan.

The Seventy Third and Seventy Fourth Constitutional Amendment Acts are the culmination of the evolutionaly process as far as secentralisation of democratic power is concerned. With passing of appropriate legislations by the state governments and the conduct of elections to the panchayati raj institutions,

Zilla parishads, Nagar Palika, etc. will be empowered to plan, fund and implement appropriate developmental works at the local level.

The Ministry of Programme Implementation (now Department of Programme implementation in the MInistry of Planning and Programme Implementation) was set up in September 1985 to usher in a new system of goaloriented management to closely monitor implementation of anti-poverty programmes, performance of all industrial infrastructure sectors of economy and implementation of Central Sector industrial projects costing over Rs. 20 crore each. The Department through its efficient system, prompt facilitative action and computerised network provided by the National Informatics Centre, is ensuring effective implementation of projects and programmes.

Infrastructure Monitoring by the Department of Programme Implementation aims at reviewing the physical performance with reference to the targets for the financial year of nine industrial infrastructure sectors namely, power, coal, steel, railways, telecommunications, shipping and ports, fertilizers, cement and petroleum and natural gas, which have a pivotal role in the economic development of the nation. This involves identifying problem areas requiring action on a priority basis and coordinating the efforts of administrative ministries with a view to overcoming critical bottlenecks, determining intersectoral linkages for achieving optimal results with emphasis on better capacity utilisation.

Physical targets (for each area in respect of each infrastructure sector) are examined at the beginning of the year for knowing the overall growth in infrastructure performance from 1985-86 to 1994-95.

The present author conducted an awareness survey with the morning and evening walkers of Vaishali and district parks of Pitampura in Delhi. Most respondents were retired teachers, government officers, businessmen and youth.

The teachers who taught economics had a fairly good idea about plans but with the exception of three or four, none had cared to read even in the newspapers about the import of the Ninth Plan approach paper. Teachers belonging to the disciplines of literature such as Hindi, Sanskrit and English had very little idea of even the concept of 'plan'.

The businessmen were more concerned with their "self-interests" and profits rather than plan/s. "The plans were the concern of Tatas and Birlas. " They were primarily concerned with the yearly budget to adjust their business accordingly.

The government officers, who retired as section officers, were hardly aware of the plan. Of course, they were concerned with their pensions and closely followed the annual budget.

The youth had hardly any time to read newspapers except about vacancies. They seemed to be a frustrated lot!

In rural India, the condition is worse. Hardly anybody knows about the plans except some of the various schemes which were advantageous to them. The common man has no knowledge or information about the plans and programmes.

Communication gap: In the absence of consciousness and awareness, it is extremely difficult to expect people to co-operate and participate in the schemes and programmes of plans. There appears to be a very big communication gap. In earlier times, "Planning Forums" in universities and colleges had made teachers and students aware of the plan/s. These should be revived. The teachers and students may take the message of plans to the people.

The funcftions of communication are, today, much wider. Besides, information and motivation, they include socialization which implies stimulation of people's active involvement in public issues. Communication has to be linked to people"s needs, both material and non-material, The mass-media, particularly the electronic media such as radio and television tend to claim a much higher degree of attention than the verbal media. This needs to be exploited fully.

Gandhi's theory of communication : Gandhi offers us a theory of non-violent communication which consists of four theoretical units. The first and foremost of theoretical units is non-violent speech and action; the second unit is the maintenance of relationships and enrichment of personality; and the third is openness; and the fourth is flexibility. Gandhi's theory of communication may be thought as instrumental in bringing about communal harmony and generating interest in the plan.

Kurukshetra : Journal of Ministry of Rural Areas and Employment can become an effective instrument of communication. Other journals such as Yojana can also play an active role in this respect.

Achievements and failures

Literacy: As per the 1991 census, the literacy rete in India was 52.11 per cent. The rate of literacy in urban male and female was 81 per cent and 63.9 per cent respectively, while in rural areas among males and females it was 57.8 per cent and 30.3 per cent respectively. The role of literacy among the Scheduled Castes and Scheduled Tribes women was pretty low i.e. 23.76 per cent and 18.19 per cent respectively.

In villages, the girl's education is far behind. If 100 girls take admision in the first grade, by the time they reach fifth standard only 40 girls remain; in the eighth standard only 18, in the 10th, 9 and only one in the twelfth standard. The picture changes radically in urban areas. There are 82 in the fifth, 62 in the eighth, 32 in the tenth and 14 in the twelfth standard.

Drinking water: There are 27 per cent villages and 21 per cent cities, where safe driking water is available. In 1,62,000 villages, no potable water is available as per the data obtained from government sources by 1993. In fact, there are 60 per cent villages which have no safe drinking water, while liquor shops are there in 90 per cent villaves.

Housing: There is a shortage of 13.7 million houses in villages according to 1991 census. The living conditions in 36 per cent in cities and 73 per cent in villages are extremely poor.

Link roads: As per oficial estimates, out of 1,29,852 villages with a population of 1,000 or more, 1,12,190 villages have links roads (1995-96). The late US President, John F. Kennedy once said : "It is not wealth that builds our roads but roads that build our wealth".

Availability of food: In 1991, per capita availability of food was 510 grams which has come down to 474.2 grams by 1994. Health: There are primary health centres in almost all the blocks of the country. Arrangement for a 30-bed hospital is made for a population of one lakh. Access to sanitation is available only to 16 per cent of the people of India.

The general difficulty recognized by all studies is that government schemes and programmes do not reach people for whom they are meant. The late Prime Minister Rajiv Gandhi had said that only 15 paise reach people out of the 100 earmarked. Thus the "citizen" is lost between leaders and bureaucrats.

Prof B.M. Bhatia şays that vaious poplist programmes although thought of as poverty alleviating and job creation programmes, are in reality nothing more than vote catching devices used by politicians to keep themselves in power. And all this at the cost of the public exchequer. They are nothing but bribes to the voters for casting the vote in favour of ruling political party or parties which initiated the programes. It is time people understood that the public distribution system (PDS), dual pricing system, consumption articles, and running multitude of welfare schemes are all part of the game politicians play in a democracy. By coing so, they are promoting their own selfish interests, and by no means serving a public cause. The UF government, though in a minority in the Lok Sabha, has started giving the impression the it will act boldly in the matter. A Cabinet Minister said the other day: "We can's seconomy". This comes as a whiff of fresh air. Besides, he went on to add, "the previous...government which sougth to be populist and held back a price hike for petrol for three years and introduced a subsidy of Rs. 1,288 crore for sugar in 1992 could not come back to power".

Micro-level planning

The Planning Commission has indicated, in the Ninth Five Year Plan that the priorities for the public sector outlays are the seven basic minimum services that were identified and adopted by the Chief Ministers' conference of July, 1996 for attainment by AD 2000. It is believed that social development and rural development cannot take place in a noon-growth environment. Employment and social security are vital to social development. Hence, the focus of micro-planning is made on:

(i) Cent per cent coverage provision of safe drinking water in rural and urban areas;

(ii) Cent per cent coverage of primary health service facilities in rural and urban areas;

(iii) Universalization of primary education;

(iv) Provision of public housing assistance to all shelterless poor families;

(v) Extension of midday meal programme in primary schools to all rural blocks and urban slums disadvantaged sections;

(vi) provision of connectivity to all unconnected villages and habitations;

(vii) Streamlining the public distribution system with the focus on the poor;

(viii) Growth and growth-related infrastructure particularly power and irrigation;

(ix) Employment; and

(x) Social security.

Thus the seven basic minimum services, growth and growth-related infrastructure, employment and social security form the focus of micro-level planning.

Planning for and by the people: Two teams comprising officials and non-officials, visit the habitations and encourage people to participate in Shramdan and also apprise them of the need for and scope of micro-level planning. The teams also help the people to draw up their own plans in all the sectors which would reflected the vision of the villagers on different key areas in their ward, the desired and achievable goals in five years, the next one year and the next quarter. It indicates the specific action by the people and identify the assistance required from the government to achieve the goals set by them. Under this exercise, the students' team led by a lecture who is a group leader would act in close co-operation with the Sarpanch and the ward members, teachers and other village functionaries, youth clubs, literacy campaign volunteers, non-government organizations, women's groups, watershed committee members, Vana Samrakshana Samithi members et al. The micro-level plan so prepared would be handed over to the nodal officer for eventual transfer to the Gram Panchayat. It is the villagers who would implement the plan for themselves and by themselves and they could do so effectively. The implementation of the programme would be reviewed periodically.

Since the launching of the Janmabhoomi programme is the first of its kind in the country, the success of the programme would lead to further effective implementation of the micro-level planning in Andhra Pradesh as well as other States. Against this background, an effort is made in the present article to evaluate the Janmabhoomi programme in Cuddapah district of Andhra Pradesh.

The study was conducted in Cuddapah, a backward drought-prone district in the Rajyalaseema region of the State. Out of 50- Mandals, 20 were randomly selected for the present study. From each selected Mandal, a sample of 15 group leaders were drawn and the primary data was collected using a pre-structured scheduled besides discussions with the nodal officers, parents and political leaders.

The Janmabhoomi programme was launched in all 2,494 habitations in Cuddapah district. The programme also covered 22 slums in Cuddapah municipality and 29 slums in Proddatur municipality. As many as 2,682 Prajala Vaddaku Palana teams were formed in addition to 2,552 roup leaders comprising lecturers, headmasters and teachers. The notable feature was the voluntary involvement of 21,337 junior and degree college students including 2,680 girls in the programme. And, the youth, voluntary organizations, political parties and leaders also enthusiastically participated in the programme. The government officials and the school teachers functioned as 2,835 facilitators to provide the required facilities to the teams and to-co-ordinate the villagers and the teams.

The group leaders and students stayed in the habitations from January 1 to 8 to serve and motivate the villagers to participate in Shramdan and improve their surroundings. Emphasis was laid on providing clean drinking water, health and hygiene, environmental cleanliness, primary education and family planning and inculcating a sense of unity and self-reliance, and enlightened people on achieving development through a positive approach. Under the health package, vitamin A was administered to children under five years of age to prevent incidence of night blindness and iron and folic doses were given to check anaemia. All the eligible couples with two children were motivated to undergo sterilization and oral contraceptive were distributed to recently married couples. The Department of Agriculture and the District Rural Development Agency also prepared packages and propagated the rural development schemes.

In the Janmabhoomi programme, the institution of Gram Sabha played a prominent role. Gram Sabhas or village meetings were conducted in the evenings where various problems were discussed. Solutions were worked out besides preparation of micro-level planning of the habitation for the next three months, one year as well as the vision statement in respect of all the sectors for the next five-year period with the help of the Sarpanch and other leaders in the villages. The team not only prepared the actual planning on the basis of locally available resources but also helped the villagers in identifying the problem areas and in planning for remedial action or further progress in different key areas. Cleaning of school premises, clearance of thorny bushes, cleaning and upkeep of sanitation, maintenance of potable water, laying of roads, digging of soakpits near hand-pumps, repairing the bore wells, white washing of school and government buildings, plantation of trees, and repairs to irrigation canals were some of the important services renders by the teams in the villages with the active participation of the public. They also sensitized the villagers on issues like health, hygiene literacy, savings, environment, etc. Besides, the students surveyed the habitations under the supervision of their group leaders and collected all the details relating to literacy, size of family, drinking water, sanitation, health care, family planning, primary education, public distribution, power, transport, roads, communication, etc. which are evolved into basic data for the future planning of the habitation with allocations coming in the next budget.

Planning is not only an instrument of economic growth but it is accepted by all that it is an instrument of social integration. Indian society consists of many social groups both in caste, community and ethnic terms. During the national movement it was realized that political mobilization has to be done in the context of the castes and community terms. That is why Gandhi is known as a political fold. Their participation fold. Their participation in the political movement brought their economic and social needs into sharp focus. Any planning has to recognize their needs. As such, the Indian Donstitution has recognized these social groups. They are socially and economically backward. They do not have access to modern education and social services. Planning as a concept was developed during the national movement. The democratic experiment of India has to take into account the needs of SCs/STs and the OBCs. It is mandatory.

Reforms

Planning is an integral part of our political culture. Strengthening democracy is possible with planning,. Planning accepts the role of State in the market economy. The role of the State is to reduce the regional disparity. It is to reduce the income disparity between various sections of our society. Liberalization process has restricted the role of the State in the area of industrialization. The private capital is today strong enough to stand on its own feet. Withdrawing the State from economic activities is a welcome step. But historical experience of the Third World countries show that the first decade of economic liberalization generated lot of economic distress. The approach paper to the Ninth Five Year Plan document has recognized this new development.

First, the regional disparity between poorer regions and richer areas has increased. Regional disparity has created already a lot of political mobilization on ethnic line.

Secondly, investment in agriculture has slowed down during this phase which sustains a majority of our people to earn their livelihood. Even after 50 years of industrialization, our agriculture is not self-sustaining. It needs State intervention for its growth. The lack of agricultural growth has reduced the employment opportunities that is reflected in the rise of unemployment and underemployment in rural India and which has pushed them to overcrowd the cities. As a result, it has increased urban poverty. Both rural and urban poverty have a close relationship.

Thirdly, urban areas are facing the crisis, in terms of providing drinking water and sanitation where the urban poor are living.

Fourthly, the decade of economic liberalization has increased the number of poor, people below the poverty line. Who are these poor people in the rural areas and urban slums? They are nobody except the people from the SCs/STs and the lower OBCs. These social classes are today the worst victims of the economic process.

The approach paper to the Ninth Plan has looked into the factors explained in the above paragraphs. It demands the reorientation of the State role and definite thrust on the poverty alleviation and employment generation without which the poor are going to distrust the democratic system. Once alienation of these communities from the system starts growing, then the system itself is going to be vulnerable.

The year 1991 marks a watershed in the economic history of India, as the country went through a paradigm shift-from one of the most highly regulated economies of the world which was essentially inward-looking to a market-oriented system, reducing the role of Government in making economic decisions, as the means to achieve higher growth of the economy and its rapid integration with the rest of the world.

An economic stabilisation programme and structural reforms covering trade, industry, taxation, financial sector and capital market were put through turning the worst economic crisis that confronted India since Independence into an opportunity to usher in a quiet revolution which would enable the country to attain a trajectory of higher growth and, along with it, social equity.

Developments in the Gulf region in 1990 exerted pressures on India's balance of payments and with outflow of capital, mainly NRI deposits, the foreign exchange reserves declined to about one billion dollars (barely two weeks of imports) in June 1991. The country was for the first time on the verge of defaulting on its external debt. There was no choice but to have recourse to a structural adjustment programme with the International Monetary Fund providing a standby credit for a stabilisation programme coupled with wide-ranging reforms.

The first steps were in the area of Trade Policy by devaluing the rupee by 22 per cent in dollar terms, eliminating export subsidy and reducing import licensing restrictions. A dual exchange rate system was ushered in but by March 1993, it was unified and a fully floating exchange rate regime in which the exchange rate is determined by market forces of demand and supply came into being. The foreign exchange market was widened and deepened, and in August 1994, the rupee was made fully convertible on current account, trade and non-trade. The downward adjustment of the rupee was designed to improve the country's international competitiveness and correct the imbalances in trade and current accounts.

Beginning with the 1991-92 Budget, Government also launched a phased reduction of import tariff bringing down the maximum from 300 per cent in 1990 to 50 per cent by march 1995. The changes resulted in lowering the import-weighted average tariff from 87 per cent in 1991 to 27 per cent in March 1995. The dispersion of tariffs was also significantly reduced and quantitiative restrictions were substantially eased. The trade reforms undertaken from 1991 helped to reduce the anti-export bias of Indian industry which was being exposed to both domestic and international competition.

The thrust of the Export-Import Policy (1992-97), made coterminus with the Eighth Five year Plan, is export promotion which is crucial for balance of payment and at the same time the Policy facilitates the import of production inputs required for sustaining increased industrial growth and exports.

Exports have responded impressively to the policy reforms and after the slowdown in the first two years under the impact of macrostabilisation measures, grew by an average of 18-19 per cent in the subsequent three years (1993-94 to 1995-96) in dollar terms. Exports have now diversified both commoditywise and countrywise with an increasing share going to the rest of Asia, particularly East and South East Asia with which India is trying to evolve increased trade and investment cooperation, given the rapid growth and the dynamism of these economies.

India's exports have undoubtedly gained from the expansion in world trade-as will be seen from the fact that a slowdown in global exports in 1996 has also effected India's exports to some extent in the current year-but the Government is confident that the export target of 38 billion dollars in 1996-97 would be achieved as against the 31.8 billion in 1995-96. A target of 75 billion dollars of exports by 2,000 A.D. has been set and this would mean maintaining an annual export growth of around 20 per cent in dollar terms over the next four years. This would facilitate a steady rise in the ratio of exports and imports in GDP and take India closer to one per cent as its share of world trade by the year 2001. Changes in the direction of India's trade from 1960-61 are brought out in Table IV.

In recent years, a largest percentage of imports are covered by exports—88 per cent in 1995-96. Imports have also increased with industry stagin a strong recovery from 1993-94 onwards to record double digitrates of growth. The higher import bill also reflects the demand for mass consumption items like pulses and edible oils apart from the growing dependence on imports of petroleum crude and products to keep pace with the rapid growth in energy use in the country.

Local resource mobilization & local planning

Indeed at the local level, resources like land, labour and human and physical resources—physical capital to a limited extent are available. Techno—economic surveys can identify the potential resources. But will all the labour force be mobilized for gainful and productive employment? This is a more important task and accompllishing ths depends on the integration of the techno—economic approach with other aspect of the social system and development process. This is the concern of many mono—disciplines like economics, engineering, sociology, psychology, etc. All such studies have pointed out that only at the local level, the basic needs, particularly of vulnerable sections can be identified and they justify larger investment in primary education for promoting health, nutrition, rural development, family size, fertility, literacy and awareness of national culture.

It is true that rural development is in the main equivalent to the development of food and cash croops and their needed inputs—irrigation, fertilizer, seeds and other resource inputs–animal husbandry, dairying and poultry farming, fisheries, forestry and agro—industries. (Dr,. Malcolm S. Adisheshiah in Bulletin of Madras Institute of Development Studies, January 1991 P.41). But such investments in agricultural developmentare bound to be more effective when there is adequate investment in human resource development, particularly in literacy and primary education. Between the I and VII Five Year Plans, there has been a decline in agriculture, forestry, animal husbandry,fisheries irrigation, rural development and village and cottage industry from Rs. 45,924.70 crore to Rs. 45,523.02 crore (ie from 54.92% to 23.62% of the total public sector outlay). But in spite of the decline in agricultural outaly, rural development culd have been quickened if only there had been more investment in human resources and human developmen. Local resource mobilization with local planning seems to be a promising vehicle for promoting rural development and alleviating poverty.

Local resource mobilization and substitution of human capital as well as physical capital is in conformity with the experience of some of the Scandinaviancountriesand Japan in this context. Theyhave been able to substitute the scarce resources with resource mobilizaton at the local level in rural and agricultural sectorsin particular. Such local resources cannot flow to higher levels but can improve productivity at the local level. This resource augmenting effect has the advatage of accelerating agricultural growth.

In such an effort, equity will have to be given special consideration. The disadvantaged population has to be seen not in therole ofobjects of participation but they are to be integrated as the subjects ofoperation. There should be also anb organizational structure which promotes the effective participation of the disadvantagedpopulation. The emergence of local bodies with elected representatives, one hopes, will make it possible to privide thisinfrastructure.

There should be sound planning at the three levels of District Panchayats, Panchayat Samithis and Village Panchayats.

In the light of the experience and achievements of the revised 20-Point Programme 1982 and the emerging new socio-economic problems during the Seventh Plan (1985-90) the programmes were restructured in 1986 with the directions given by the then Prime Minister Shri Rajiv Gandhi which was popularly known as 20-Point Programme 1986. The restructured programmes came into effect from 1 April 1987 along with Annual Plan of 1987-88. Briefly, the programmes are as under:

— Attack on Rural Poverty: (i) ensure that poverty alleviation programmes reach all the poor in every village; (ii) dovetail wage employment programmes with programmes for area development and human resource development and create national and community assets like school buildings, roads, tanks, fuel and fodder reserves; (iii) correlate the various rural development productivity and production-expand rural employment; (iv) promote handlooms, handicrafts, village and small industries and improve skills for self-employment; and (v) Revitalise Panchayats, cooperatives and local bodies.

— Strategy for Rain-fed Agriculture: (i) improve the technology for conserving moisture and ensure better management of land and water resources; (ii) develop and distribute appropriate and improved seeds; and (iii) reduce vulnerability to drought through suitable changes in droughtprone areas and drought-relief programmes.

— Better use of Irrigation Water: (i) Develop the catchment areas and improve drainage in basins and deltas; (ii) improve irrigation management in command areas; (iii) prevent water logging, salinity and wasteful use; and (iv) coordinate the use of surface and ground water

— Bigger Harvests: (i) revolutionise rice production in the eastern region and other areas of low productivity; (ii) achieve self-reliance in edible oils; (iii) secure greater production of pulses; (iv) intensify the cultivation of fruits and vegetables; (v) augment facilities for modern storage, processing and marketing of agricultural produce; (vi) help livestock and dairy framers to increase productivity; and (vii) develop fish farming and sea fishing.

— Enfrocement of Land Reforms: (i) complete compilation of land records; (ii) implement agricultural land ceilings; and (iii) distribute surplus land to the landless.

— Special Programmes for Rural Labour: (i) enforce minimum wages for unorganised labour in agriculture and industry, (ii) fully implement laws abolishing bonded labour; and (iii) involve voluntary agencies in prigrammes for the rehabilitation of bonded labour.

— Clean Drinking Water: (i) provide safe water all villages; (ii) assist local communities to maintain the sources of such water supply in good condition; (iii) pay special attention to water supply for SCs and STs.

— Health for All: (i)Improve the quality of primary health care; (ii) fight leprosy, TB malaria, goitre, blindness and other major diseases; (iii) provide immunisation for all infants and children; (iv) improve sanitation facilities in rural areas, particularly for women; and (v) pay special attention to programmes for the rehabilitation of the handicapped.

— Two Child Norm: (i) bring about voluntary acceptance ofthe two child norm; (ii) promote responsible parenthood; (iii) reduce infant mortality; and (iv) expand maternity and child care facilities.

— Expansion of Education: (i) universalise elementary education with special emphasis on girls' education; (ii) improve the content of education at all levels; (iii) promote non-formal education and functional literacy programmes, including promotion of skills; (iv) stimulate adult literacy programmes, with the participation of students and voluntary agencies; and

(v) emphasis on national integration and social and moral values and instil pride in our heritage.

— Justice to Scheduled Castes and Scheduled Tribes: (i) ensure compliance with the constitutional provisions and laws for the SCs and STs; (ii) ensure possession of land allotted to SCs and STs; (iii) revitalise the land allotment programme; ()iv) organise and assist special coaching programmes to immprove educational standards, (v) eradicate scavenging and undertake special programmes for the rehabilitation of Safai Karamcharis; (vi) provide better direction and adequate funds for the special component programmes; (vii) pursue programmes for the fuller integration of SCs and STs with the rest of the society; and (viii) ensure the rehabilitation of tribals displaced from their habitat.

— Equality for Women: (i) raise the status of women; (ii) enhance awareness of the problems of women; (iii) create mass consciousness about women's rights; (iv) implement a national programme of training and employment for women; (v) enable women to participate with equality in socio-economic development and nation-building; and (vi) rouse public opinion against dowry and ensure effective implementation of anti-dowry legislation.

— New Opportunities for Youth: (i) enlarge opportunities for youth in sports, adventure and cultural activities; (ii) promote physical fitness; (iii) involve youth on a massive scale in projects of national development such as the cleaning of the Ganga, the conservation and enrichment of the environment and mass education; (iv) identify outstanding young persons in all fields to encourage and develop their talents; (v) involve youth in temper; (vi) expand the network of Nehru Yuvak

Kendras; (vii) strengthen the National Service Scheme and the National Cadet Corps; and (viii) encourage voluntary agencies working for the welfare of rural youth.

— Housing for the People: (i) make available house sites to the rural poor; (ii) expand programmes of house construction; (iii) lay special emphasis on construction of houses for SCs and STs; and (iv) develop low cost building materials.

— Improvement of Slums: (i) restrict the growth of slums; (ii) provide basic facilities in existing slum areas; and (iii) encourage planned house building in urban areas.

— New Strategy for Forestry: (i) grow more trees and raise more firest, with the full involvement of the people; (ii) protect the traditional rights of tribal populations and local communities of access to fuel wood and forest produce; (iii) reclaim wastelands for productive use; and (iv) plant appropriate vegetation in hilly, desert and coastal areas.

— Protection of the Environment: (i) enhance public awareness of the dangers of environmental degradation; (ii) mobilise popular support for environmental protection; (iii) promote recognition that enduring development demands preservation of the ecology; and (iv) ensure judicious site selection for projects and proper choice of technology.

— Concern for the Consumers: (i) bring essential consumption goods within easy reach of the poor; (ii) build a consumer protection movements; (iii) restructure the distribution system so that subsidies reach the most needy; and (iv) strengthen the public distribution system.

— Energy for the Villages: (i) expand the supply of electricity for productive use in the villages; (ii) develop alternative sources of energy, particularly biogas; and (iii) promote integrated area specific programmes for rural energy.

— A Responsive Administration: (i) simplify procedures; (ii) delegate authority; (iii) enforce accountablility; (iv) evolve monitoring systems from block to national level; and (v) attend promptly and sympatherically to public grievances.

While the restructured 20-Point Programme renewed the nation's commitment to eradicate poverty, it laid balanced emphasis on how to raise overall procductivity, reduce income inequalties and remove social and economic disparities so that the ultimate fruits of development resulted in improvement of quality of life of human environment. The coverage of the programme was broadened to bring within its ambit a number of lmajor areas of social concern for fulfiling not only the 'basic needs' like adeauate provison of food, clean drinking water, housing and health facilities, it laid more emphasis on human dignity and individual rights by encouraging 'responsible' parenthood, equality for women, opportunities for the youth, rights of consumers, justice to scheduled castes and scheduled tribes, etc. The inherent philosophy behind the restructured programme was that the development has no real meaning without human dignity and individual rights.

The Government was not content with mere re-establishment of law and order. It was keen that the new sense of national purpose should be harnessed to a speedier promotion of economic growth and social justice. On 1 July, 1975, the Prime Minister announced in a nationwide broadcast a "Twenty-Point Economic Programme" designed to achieve speedy development and to remove many of the evil practices which and persisted all these years, including bonded labour and rural indebtedness. It gave a further fillip to the official drive to contain inflation and root out black money. The programme was acclaimed by all sections of the people notably farmers and landless workers, industrial workers, representatives of trade and industry, and students and teachers. This meant:

— Continuance of steps to bring down prices of essential commodities. Streamlined production, procurement and distribution of essential commodities. Strict economy in government expenditure.

— Implementation of agricultural land ceilings and speedier distribution of surplus land compilation of land records.

— Stepping up of provision of house sites for landless and weaker sections.

— Bonded labour, wherever it exists, will be declared illegal.

— Plan for liquidation of rural indebtedness. Legislation for moratorium on recovery of debt from landless labourers, small farmers and artisans.

— Review of laws on minimum agricultural wages.

— Five million more hectares to be brought under irrigation. National programme for use of underground water.

— An accelerated power programme. Super thermal stations under central control.

— New development plan for development of handloom sector.

— Improvement in quality and supply of people's cloth.

— Socialisation of urban and urbanisable land. Ceiling on ownership and possession of vacant land and on plinth area of new dwelling units.

— Special squads for valuation of conspicuous construction and prevention of tax evasion. Summary trails and deterrent punishment of economic offenders.

— Special legislation for confiscation of smugglers' properties.

— Liberalisation of investment procedures. Action against misuse of import licences.

— New schemes for workers' association of industry.

— National permit schemes for road transport.

— Income Tax relief to middle class; exemption limit placed at Rs. 8,000.

— Essential commodities at controlled prices to students in hostels.

— Books and stationery at contolled prices.

— New apprenticeship scheme to enlarge employment and training, especially of weaker sections.

Farm agencies to adopt 50,000 families—transfer of technology

Involvement of all the 860 institutions and agencies of the Indian Council of Agricultural Research (ICAR), agricultural universities and voluntary agencies for the transfer of farm techniques to the field level with adoption of 50,000 agricultural families in the programme, has been recommended by the ICAE national workshop on transfer of technology programme for rural development.

The three-day workshop has also decided to prepare a "lab to land operational manual" providing information on all available technologies, besides embarking upona continuous monitoring and evaluation of the implementation of the programme for making midcourse corrections. Such a manual will pay special attention to the small and marginal farmers and provide viable technology to them.

The workshop has decided that while ICAR and its agencies and the agricultural universities and their centres should adopt 20,000 farmers each, the voluntary organisations and affiliated agricultural college could be entrusted with the task of adopting 10,000 families.

The workshop felt that in selecting centres, preference should be given to institutions already involved in agricultural development and the selection of blocks, villages, farm families should also be preferably from the intensive agricultural development blocks already identified.

The approach for the transfer of technology should be on a cluster-village basis and proximity of the implementing agency should also be borne in mind for effective supervision.

Another important recommendation of the workshop was that related programmes for farm youth, farm women and children should be taken up simultaneously. It also strongly recommended creation of suitable marketing infrastructure and facilities well in advance to match the anticipated increased production.

The workshop recommended organisation of agricultural exhibitions at national, State, institute and university levels, during the national extension fortnight celebrations—inter-State and inter-regional exchanges, lectures by farm-professors organisation of debates and discussions special programmes and features on the radio, television, press and extension lectures should be taken up during the fortnight, it said.

Monitoring and evaluation

The departments/ministries concerned on the subject of 20-Point Programme, 1986 set the annual targets in consultation with the states and the Department of Programme Implementation (DPI). DPI monitors the implementation of the 20-Point Programme. The management information system developed by this Department for implementation of the programmes consists of (i) Monthly Progress Report; (ii) Capsule Report; (iii) Half Yearly Progress Report; and (iv) Annual Report.

Under 20-Point Programme-1986, there are 119 items identified for monitoring. Of these, 54 are monitored on an evaluatory basis and 65 items are retained for physical targetting/monitoring. Again of the 65 items identified for quantitative assessment, 28 items have been identified for monitoring on a monthly basis. Only 19 items, out of the 28 items of the Monthly Report, are taken for the purpose of ranking. The Half Yearly Report covers majority of the items of 20-Point Programme indicating qualitative performance.

A three-tier system of monitoring has been established in the states/UTs, as follows: (a) at the agency level which are entrusted with the execution of the programmes in the field level; (b) at the state level which provides infrastructure and direction for programme execution; and (c) at the Central Government level not only by the sectoral ministries and departments but also by the Department of Programme Implementation under the Ministry of Planning and Programme Implementation, which oversees the monitoring and evaluation system on a contiuous basis and reports to the Cabinet Secretriat and the Prime Minister's Office.

The concern for human poverty and its eradication to improve human environment have been the central focus of our development planning in the country since the inception of the planing era. Various schemes have been formulated and implemented with the sole objective of removing poverty and thereby increasing the quality of life of the people in the lower ranks of population. The explicit manifestation of the government's concern for poverty alleviation got its expression when the first 20-Point Programme was launched on 1 July 1975 under the connotation of *Ganibi Hatao* which was conceived by the late Prime Minister Smt Indira Gandhi. This programme was implemented with a pragmatic success during 1975-76 and 1976-77 Annual Plans. The Sixth Five Year Plan (1980-85)) incorporated these programmes as guiding factors in the planning process. Taking the past experience, the original 20-Point Programme was further re-defined, revitalized and announced to the Nation on 14 January 1982.

Objectives

Increase irrigation potential, develop and dissemiinate technologies and imputs for dry land agriculture; (ii) Make special efforts to increase production of pulses and vegetable oilseeds;

Strengthen and expand coverage of integrated rural development and national rural employment programmes; (iv) Implement agricultural land ceilings, distribute surplus land and complete compilation of land records by removing all administrative and legal obstacles; (v) Review and effectively enforce minimum wages for agricultural labour; (vi) Rehabilitate bonded labour; (vii) Accelerate programmes for the development of scheduled castes and scheduled tribes; (viii) Supply drinking water to all problem villages; (ix) Allot house sites to rural families who are without them and expand programmes for construction assistance to them; (x) Improve the environment of slums, implement programmes of house building for economically weaker sections and take measures to arrest unwarranted increase in land prices; (xi) Maximise power generation, improve the functioning of electricity authorities and electrify all villages; (xii) Pursue vigorously programmes of afforestation social and farm forestry and the development of bio-gas and other alternative energy sources; (xiii) Promote family planning on a voluntary basis as a people's movement; (xiv) Substantially augment universal primary health care facilities and control of leprosy, TB and blindness; (xv) Accelerate programmes of welfare for women and children and nutrition programmes for pregnant women, nursing mothers and children, specially in tribal hill and backward areas; (xvi) Spread universal elementary education for the age group 6-14 with special emphasis on girls and simultaneously involve students and voluntary agencies in programmes for the removal of adult illiteracy; (xvii) Expand the public distribution system through more fair price shops, including mobile shops in far flung areas and shops, to cater to industrial workers, students' hostels, and make available to students textbooks and exercise books on a priority basis and to promote a strong consumer protection movement; (xviii) Liberalise investment procedures and streamline industrial policies to ensure timely completion of projects. Give handicrafts, handlooms, small and village industries all facilities to grow and to update their technology; (xix) Continue strict action against smugglers, hoarders and tax evaders and tax evaders and check black money; and (xx) Improve the working of the public enterprises by increasing efficiency, capacity utilisation and the generation of internal sources.

Various programmes were formulated to achieve the above objectives focussing mostly on the critical socio-economic constraints on development. The existence of human poverty was considered the single most adverse constraints to human development. Therefore, breaking the vicious circle of poverty which was both the cause and the effect of under development in the country was central to the formulation of 20-Point Programme. The Sixth Five Year Plan was designed taking note of the micro-objectives of 20-Point Programme in the critical sectors which were accorded high priority in the planning process. The emphasis on agricultural productivity, rural employment, provision of safe drinking water, allotment of houses sites to the rural families, improvement of slums, voluntary family planning, provision of basic health care, concern for environmental degradation, spread of elementary education, accelerating welfare programmes for the women and children were the most positive features of the revised 20-Point Programme which were spelt out keeping in view the basic objective of the development planning that the fruits of planning mustensure the 'basic needs' of human beings if development process is at all to be sustainable.

While the various evaluation reports indicate different positive impacts, the major impact of the 20-Point Programme in the country was the re—distribution of productive assets in favour of the less privileged who are the backbone of the economy. From the point of view of a sustainable growth, these programmes not only improve the productivity in the rural sector but also increased the overal quality of life in the villages to a perceptible degree.

Community initiatives & people's participation

It is evident from the above discussion that the Panchayats have been denied the possibility of carrying out participatory planning for local development at the grass roots level. This vacuum has been filled by the voluntary efforts of the people with the participation of intellectuals and voluntary network organizations like the Kerala Sastra Sahitya Parishad, Bharat Vigyan Samithi. The results of their efforts have been remarkable. In the field of literacy, the "Erankulam model" is acclaimed across the world and replicated elsewhere in India. The alphabet literacy has provided a sound base for a mass initiative in the field of environment protection, gender equality and women's empowerment. Thus social development in Kerala has been the contribution of an awakened and vigilant public. Majumdar (1995) rightly observed that "The enlightened and politically conscious electorate in Kerala closely monitors the functioning of schools, including those in the rural areas. Here, cases of shirking on the part of teachers evoke strong collection protest (e.g. many such cases are immediately publicised through posters in public places), and as a corollary, elicit appropriate policy responses.

The expansion of literacy has given a sound base for participatory planning which has successfully been operationalised in Kalliasseri Panchayat in Kannur district of the State.

The Community Development Society (CDS), with its thrift and credit activities, has improved the lot of poor women in urban Kerala. The Alappuzha CDS is an example, where "poor women have mobilized up to Rs. 37 lakh from their own savings. In two years, the Alappuzha CDS has generated more than 4,000 jobs ensuring 100 per cent loan recovery and repayment to banks as on date". Due to this exemplary work, the Alappuzha model has received "We the People Award" in 1994 from the United Nations.

Although Kerala could not provide a successful

model for participatory planning through Panchayats due to political instability, its people, with the help of dedicated voluntary organizations have offered one. The other States could benefit from its success stories in participatory planning.

Development is the primary concern and responsibility of the people. They must prepare the plan and implement the same. This is much more true with the introduction of Panchayati Raj. The voluntary organizations may also be actively involved in this task. People are the primary concern. It is their confidence and credibility that needs to be obtained. It is mutual trust between government and the people that will repose faith in each other. There are three basic principles of people-centred development. First, sovereignty resides with the people. Second, to exercise their sovereignty and assume responsibility for their own development and that of their communities, people must control their own resources, have access to relevant information, and have the means to hold the officials of government and voluntary organizations accountable. Third, those who would assist people with their development must recognize that it is they who are participating in support of the people's agenda, not vice-versa. The value of the outsider's contribution will be measured in terms of the enhanced capacity of the people to determine their own future.

The Gandhian model of development requires active involvement and participation of man building his own "destiny". This is possible if some of us belonging to the so-called rich and middle class voluntarily, instead of dfrifting toward consumerism, are willing to sacrifice and share our pleasures in the interests of the downtrodden of our society. For rural India, time is running out and it must adopt strategies and methods to transform the socio-economic life of people to suit Indian ingenuity and culture. Integrated development sets forth a strategy of working with rural people—a strategy, in which participation by all is both the means and end itself.

In sum, the real wealth of a country lies in "human capital" and if you create conditions where human capital can flourish without being squashed by government controls, you can beat the rest of the countries of the Ninth Plan has to be very positive in building up "social capital" and infrastructure. Our social achievements are not outstanding despite our fifty years of Independence. Our literacy rate is 52 per cent; infant mortality 74 per thousand; access to sanitation is available to only 16 per cent of the people. Though life expectancy has gone up to 62, the fertility rate is still 3.3 which would double India's population in the next century. Just as the proof of the pudding is in the eating, similarly the success of the Ninth Plan will depend on as to how far it has raised "human capotal" of India.

We have to shift the paradigm of development from a right centred-economy to a duty motivated economy, from self-centredness to the love of our fellowmen, if we want to succeed in our planned development of rural society.

Participatory planning

We have seen that Panchayats in Kerala have not become a viable and pulsating institution for ensuring participatory planning. The prime mover in this sphere has been the voluntary sector, But after the 73rd Constitutional Amendment which, among other things, has ensured regular elections to the Panchayats and reservation of seats as well as of posts of Chairpersons for the weaker sections at all the tiers, they have to assume this role. The elections to these institutions were also held last year.

The People's Campaign for the formulation of the Ninth Plan has also been launched in the State for making decentralized Planning the key input in preparing the State Plan. All these efforts on the part of the State government are in the right direction. But the main question is whether the Panchayats have really emerged as institutions of self-government (as envisaged in Article 243 G of the Constitution) to help materialize participatory planning. As mentioned earlier, the two important dimensions of the people's participation are: who are the people and how would the participation occur. The answer to the first question is given by M.A. Oommen (1991) while discussing the formulation of a methodology for district planning with people's participation in Kannur district where he says, by people we mean those below the poverty line. The poor people, including other marginalized sections of society, have been statutorily given berth in Panchayats. The second question is also answered by constituting the Panchayats in the State.

But the most important question regarding realization of the objective of participatory planning is whether people enjoy autonomy in their actions. In other words, whether the various provisions of the State Panchayat Act establish Panchayats as an Institution of Self-government (ISG), i.e. whether they have institutional existence, institutional capacity and financial viability. Therefore, the question discussed in this part of the paper is whether the various provisions of the Kerala Panchayat Act enable Panchayats to usher in participatory planning. And if not, what amendments need to be made.

Financial autonomy

Autonomy of people's actions which is the basis for participatory planning can only be operationalized if Panchayats enjoy financial autonomy. Let us examine the provisions of the Kerala Panchayat Raj Act to see to what extent they obstruct the exercise of this autonomy and how financial autonomy can be provided to them.

— Imposition of particular tax or levy or cess should be compulsory. If a tax is not compulsory, it could not be an effective instrument in the hands of the Panchayats to mobilise finance. For example, house tax is compulsory in Andhra Pradesh and Haryana and optional in Uttar Pradesh. Because of its mandatory nature, it has yielded more finance in Andhra Pradesh and Haryana than in Uttar Pradesh. In the Kerala Panchayati Raj Act, powers to collect fixed fees (Section 198), building tax, profession tax, advertisement tax and entertainment tax (Section 200) are not mandatory for exercise by the Panchayats. Hence, the should be made as such.

— Under the Act, rates of the cess shall be governed the rules made by the government. After repealing this provision, the Panchayats should be empowered to decide the rate of a particular cess.

— The scope for imposing taxes should also be enlarged. In this regard, Panchayats should be empowered to auction river sand, levy fee on quarrying and for pumping water from canals etc.

— A provision should also be made in the Act that if a lower tier of Panchayat is unable to perform the assigned functions, the next higher tier shall examine the problem and help it out. Besides, helping out the lower tier of Panchayat, this will also establish an organic link between the different tiers. One of the important features of the Gujarat Panchayat (TP) shall provide resources to enable it to perform its functions effectively (Section 204).

— The Karnataka Panchayat Act provides for

arrangement of grant for the GP under which a grant of Rs. 1 lakh is to be provided by the State government. This amount shall be used to meet electricity charges, maintenance of water supply scheme, etc. of the GP (Section 208). No other State has made this kind of a provision for GPs, Kerala should also have such a provision in its Panchayat Act.

— There must be a separate head for Panchayats in the State budget. This head should include share from tax and non-tax revenue, grant-in-aid and resources allocated to Panchayats for performing agency functions.

— As per Section 214 (7) of the Act, the Village Panchayats and Block Panchayats shall submit their budgets to the Panchayat, which along with its budget submit them to the government. This is against the letter and spirit of local government. Budgets passed by the VPs should go the BP which after consolidating them should submit them to the DP. The DP, instead of sending them to the government, should submit the budget of this whole rular area to the District Planning Committee which, after consolidating the plans of rural and urban areas should submit it to the State government.

— In order to examine and scrutinize the accounts of the Panchayats, West Bengal has constituted a District Council comprising the largest recognized political party in the opposition its Chairperson, one Vice-Chairperson and five other members to be elected by the members of the DP and three government officers nominated by the government. A similar provision may also be adopted by Kerala for financial discipline of the Panchayats.

— The MPs' Local Area Development Scheme which is implemented by Distict Collectors may be implemented through Panchayats and municipalities, because items of works of this scheme are almost similar to the XI Schedule of the Constitution. If this is done, it will not only help in according financial autonomy to the local government but also lessen spatial gaps in various social infrastructures. When this scheme was introduced in Parliament, only the left parties objected to it on the plea that it went against the spirit of decentralization. In Kerala, where the same parties are now in power, they should how the political Panchayats and the municipalities.

Constitution and composition of panchayats

Not giving membership to MPs and MLAs in Panchayats, not tampering with the VP and Block Panchayats (BPs) boundaries for the membership of the BPs and the District Panchayat, (DP) respectively and making the Chairpersons of the lower tier members of the immediate upper tier for establishing an organic link among them are welcome features of the State Act, which should also be emulated by other States. But there are certain features of the Act which need to be amended as they are against the spirit of the Central Act and participatory planning. These are:

— In Chapter II of the Act, reorganization of the boundaries of the wards of Panchayats has been vested in the State government, which is against the provisions of Articles 243 k and 243 O of the Constitution. All functions pertaining to the delimitation of boundaries, including disputes between or among Panchayats, should be performed by the State Election Commission.

- A provision for reservation of OBCs should also be made in the Act to enable them to participate effectively in decentralized governance.
- The election of the Chairperson of the VP should be made direct as is the case in most States. In this way, the Chairperson will be able to draw authority from the people. Besides making Chairpersons accountable to the people, this will also strengthen the institution of the GS.
- To provide more space for weaker sections to participate in planning and development, the reservation for SCs, STs, OBCs and women should be extended to include the post of Vice-Chairperson of different tiers. At present, Punjab is the only State where such a provision has been made at the intermediate and apex tiers. Kerala may do well to go one step further and provide reservation for these sections at all tiers of the Panchayats.
- As per Section 151 of the Act, if the government is satisfied that a Panchayat at any level cannot be constituted for certain reasons, like failure to elect the majority of the members, it can appoint an Administrative Committee consisting of at least the elected members and a President and Vice-President, or appoint a special officer for period not exceeding six months. This provision is against the spirit of the Constitution. If such an eventuality arises, only the elected representatives should govern the Panchayats for a specified period and not a special officer. Therefore, the provision of a special officer provided in this section should be deleted.

Functional autonomy

Devolving of adequate and clear-cut functions and powers to the Panchayats is very important for enabling them to function in a free environment. Let us examine the scope of Kerala Panchayat Raj Act (KPRA) in this regard.

— Under Section 164 (2), a provision has been made for constituting a Ward Committee for each constituency with the purpose of informing the VP on the needs of the constituency. But the GS will also be held at the ward level only, which among others, will list out its needs as is also envisaged as the role of the Ward Committee. The VP may also constitute a vigilance Committee as suggested earlier in this paper. Keeping these provisions in view, constitution of the Ward Committee is dispensable.

— The District panchayats, Block Panchayats and Village Panchayats shall perform their functions under the financial and technical guidance of the State government [Sections 166 (2), 172 (2) 173 (2)]. This is wrong in principle and operationally difficult as it does not put Panchayats on a firm foundation. Through provisions of this nature, the government can meddle with the functioning of the democratically elected institutions and deprive the people of freedom of action which is essential for participatory planing.

These provisions in the State Act may have to be suitably amended so that the VP takes help from the BP which, in turn, takes help from the DP and the DP from the State government, if it is required. The State may be benefited from the Panchayati Raj Acts of States like Gujarat, Assam, Manipur and Madhaya Pradesh which have enabling provisions for consultation among the three tires without much intervention from the State.

— Functions to be performed by different tiers of Panchayats have been listed in Schedules 3,4 and 5 of the Act. Looking at their distribution among the three tiers, an hour glass picture emerges, because they have been concentrated either at the lowest level or at the apex. This shows that in deciding the distribution, proper thought has not been given. For example, functions relating to education do not figure in the list for the BP, which thus emerges as a weak tier of the PR system and, therefore, does not provide sufficient scope for its members to play a role in participatory planning.

While participating in the Conference of Chief Ministers on basic minimum services 4-5, July, 1996 in Delhi, the Chief Minister of Kerala mentioned that less than one per cent of the total habitations in the State were fully covered as regards the availability of safe drinking water against the national coverage of 57 per cent. Shortage of clean drinking water is an important reason for the high morbidity in the State. This is one of the basic needs and could be handled effectively at Panchayat level. But very little responsibility to this basic necessity has been devolved to the Panchayats. It is suggested that in order to conserve water resources, construction of check dams in the rivers should be entrusted to the Panchayats. If this function is given lock stock and barrel to the Panchayats, it being a basic requirement, will enthuse the people to participate in water management.

— In inter-tier allocation of functions, the cardinal principle that what can be undertaken at a particular level should be entrusted to that level alone has been kept in mind. However, ample scope for improving the functional relationship between the three tiers is still there. Significantly, whatever functions have been allocated to the Panchayats in accordance with this principle have been taken away by Section 283, according to which the government may alter, amend or add to any of the entries made in the functions of the Panchayats. Hence this section should be repealed.

— To fully realize economic development and social justice, other functions like police powers and judicial powers should also be given to the Panchayats. Bihar, West Bengal, Punjab and Uttar Pradesh are the States which have given judicial functions to institutions at the grass roots level. Recently, the Madhya Pradesh State Assembly has also passed a legislation for constituting Gram Nyayalayas to administer justice in rural areas. The Karnataka government also proposes to introduce an amendment to the State's Panchayat Act in the coming session of the Assembly for setting up Nyaya Panchayats. The kerala Panchayat Raj Act does not make provision for constituting Nyayalaya at grass roots levels for dispensing justice to the people. It is, therefore, suggested that police and judicial functions should be given to the Panchayats for meaningful decentralization.

Functional autonomy has not been given to the Panchayats, because provisions such as the schemes being contingent on the availability of resources and placing of performance of vital functions under the supervision and guidance of the government have circumscribed the role of participatory planning through the institutions. For ushering in an era of participatory planning for Panchayats, the State government should amend all the Acts pertaining to the subjects in the XIth Schedule of the Central Act, take out all relevant portions from the existing Subjects Acts and incorporate them in the Panchayat Act through an amendment by the State legislature.

Administrative autonomy

For enabling the people to participate effectively in planning and development of their areas through Panchayats, it is indispensable that these bodies should have their own officials. But this has not been provided for in the Kerala Panchayat Act.

— The secretaries of all the three tiers will be the government employees (Section 179) under the State Act. The power of transferring these employees is also vested in the government or in a prescribed authority if a resolution to that effect has been passed by the Panchayat by a simple majority. However, action on this resolution is not mandatory on the part of the government. This provision is objectionable, because this does not entail autonomy of the people in their actions. What is the rationale behind insisting on a simple majority for a resolution for transferring an official? It is practised at the State and the Central levels? Hence this provision may have to be repealed.

— The Chairpersons of the Panchayats have been empowered to exercise supervision and control over the officials of the Panchayats and prepare their confidential reports (Section 156 (4) (b). It is a welcome feature of the Act. But provisions in the Kerala Munidipal Act [Section 14 (3) (b)] which say that Chairpersons prepare the confidential report of the Secretary as well as review the confidential reports prepared by the Secretaries in respect of their employees should also be made applicable to the Panchayats.

— An enabling provision for constituting a separate Service or Cadre [Section 179 (3)] has been made in the Act. Other States which have some such provisions are Karnataka [Section 196 (5) and Punjab

(Section 26). But the provision in the Kerala Act is not substantial in nature as it has not been clearly specified as has been done in the Gujarat Panchayati Raj Act. The provision under Section 179 (3) of the KPRA must be operationalized at once so that the Panchayats have their own officers and employees. Kerala may be benefited from Gujarat and Rajasthan Panchayati Raj Acts in which provisions for Panchayat cadre have already been incorporated. Under the Gujarat Panchayati Raj Act, there will be three cadres of Panchayat employees, namely the District cadre, the Taluk cadre and the Local cadre [Section 227 (3)]. For this purpose, a Gujarat Panchayat Service Selection Board shall be constituted. Besides this Board, a District Panchayat Service Selection Committee shall also be constituted at the district-level to recruit the primary education staff (Section 236). In Rajasthan, a provision for establishing a District Establishment Committee under the chairpersonship of the President of the ZP has been made. This Committee shall make selections for the posts in different grades and categories for the Panchayats, prepare lists of the persons for promotion and deal with disciplinary matters affecting the officers and employee except officers of the State cadre.

Actually, a permanent solution of the cadre problem is to amend the Constitution, because the Panchayats after becoming local government must have their own employees as the State and the Centre have as per part XIV of the Constitution. But to begin with, the State government must invoke immediately the enabling provisions in the Panchayat Act.

Modern planning

Whether it is fully realized or not, the Ninth Plan planning represents a new age planning of an age of management culture, economic restructuring, resource scarcity, economy, value for investment, global competition, MNCs, mega investments, free trade, intellectual property rights, R & D, productivity, quality, efficiency, hardware and software of production, human capital, strategic planning, economic vision, government-private sector partnership, value by results, international capital, regional economic groupings, delicensing, decentralization, lean taxation, FDI, foreign borrowings, JVs, market pricing, opening of the economies, public-private sector parity or equality, fiscal discipline, public-orientation, deregulations, budgetary imbalances, de-nationalisation, corporate takeovers, subsidy-cuts, commercialization of agriculture and free trade in agricultural goods, non-farm enterprises in rural areas, entrepreneurship, innovations, paid lunches, cutting down free rides, user-charges, gender equality and empowerment of women, and soon.

Break from the past: In spite of its not insignificant achievements, the bane of Indian planning has been poor implementation and results, viz operational shortcomings and 'targetism'. The Ninth Plan should and ought to make a break from it, to justify its nearly Rs. 1 crore investiment. It must have multiple effect, without which it is bad planning, though the plans do not work out the multipliers. The plan has to learn a leaf or two from corporate planning, particularly of MNCs which mean business of every dollar of investment. Not that the Plan should be devoid of human concerns and values, which it or for that matter any public planning anywhere should be responsive to, given the concern of planning with the have-nots. That is, the results of the planning need be measured not only, by the hard facts of growth rate but also by the light and laughter in the lives of the common people, visible to the naked eye. Otherwise, the purpose of the whole planning exercise would be much lost.

Meeting the challenge: All said and done, the fact should be brought home to the planners in the Ninth Plan that it requires a lot of suffering and sacrifice to make the Plan operative with so much investment and it should yield commensurate returns in health, education, employment, social infrastructure, economic overheads, employment, enterprises, etc. for which the Plan is intended. India is one of the most poverty-ridden and low income countries. Our per capita income is not even $ 400 per annum. Millions and millions of people's daily concerns water, sanitation, medical aid, food and employment. Accordingly, the new age planning consists of making plan investments go as far as possible or maximum yielding. Planning must make the deserts bloom, not allow the forests to vanish so to say. If not, it is not proper planning.

Whether the plan size is optimal, suboptimal or overoptimal is irrelevant in the context of the plan. From plan-to-plan, planning efforts anyhow need to be raised. Considering This the plan is not at all oversized, considering the magnitude of the problems facing the economy and the efforts needed to overcome them. It is a different thing if the nation opts for a soft and small Ninth Plan. At no time, the plans had escaped the label of being ambitious and oversized. Notwithstanding plan size, the basic economic problems remain intact, if the poverty-line population increasing recently to 37 per cent is any indication.

An opportune time: Only, the Ninth Plan should be a new age planning or plan of operational efficiency, economy, efficiency, discipline, human and grass roots development, competitive, forward looking, co-ordinating and comprehensive. In addition, it must be time and cost bound. No doubt, it is a tall order of things but it is unavoidable if the Ninth Plan is to spell a success and make a dent into the thousand problems of the economy and the people. We have been lethargic with planning and it is time to be strictly business and management minded about planning and plan and the Ninth Plan is the right and opportune time to commence new age planning, without which it becomes increasingly difficult to sustain planning.

That is the law of diminishing returns which appears to have set in planning, since long, needs to be reversed in the Ninth Plan, failing which zero and even negative marginal productivities may set in for plan investments. There are increasing constraints on plan resources due to which the Ninth Plan should successfully go through its arithmetic of investments and returns in different lines of production and try to realize them for the first time in planning history of the country in tune with the new age stress on returns rather than or just investments. The Ninth Plan, in other words, should incorporate into its functioning strict business principles. The Plan thus should open a new chapter in planning not only in India but also the world over. Planning should assert itself and march ahead in the so-called market ruled economy and dispense its benefits to its large multitudes standing second to none in economy, efficiency and execution. It is the mandate of the populace. There is a national consensus behind planning, particularly the Ninth Plan, which promises to be a plan of action and of the people. It promises to give thrust to the thrust areas. Economy, productivity, returns and people should be the watchwords of new planning to commence with the Ninth Plan. There is no activity commensurate in importance with the Plan that should be No. 1 programmes, as nothing involves such a massive investment and the welfare and happiness of millions and millions of people and their living and natural environment.

One has to harp at length about the need for new planning because of the debris that is being left behind by improper planning, which is downward rather than upward. Rural development, for instance, is a greatly neglected aspect of our planning and the Ninth Plan promises to remove the whole backlog of it including human resource development and women and child development. Great challenges lay ahead of the new planning process.

According to Prof Madhu Dandavate, Deputy Chairman of the Planning Commission, the Ninth Plan accords "the highest priority to generating adequate productive employment, eradication of poverty, focus on agriculture and rural development with emphasis on radical land reforms".

Power—Crucial Infrastructure: Pointing out that the power sector constitutes the most crucial infrastructure both for agriculture and industry, he said that the problems of power must be carefully handled in a co-ordinated fashion with due attention for the proper choice of fuels, the adequacy of their availability, the need to rationalize tariff structure, and to prevent transmission and distribution losses.

In fact, the problem of power may reach crisis proportions in the next few years unless urgent action is taken by every state. The financial, managerial and administrative structue of State Electricity Boards (SEBs) and their policies must be changed dramatically and urgently so that the Electricity Boards can raise tariffs to realistic levels, improve the quality of supply, contain power theft and become financially viable. The Finance Minister, Mr. P. Chidambaram, is of the view that the Central and State laws need to be changed to allow SEBs and private electricity companies to function autonomously subject to independent regulatory authorities.

Agricultural Growth: In respect of sectoral strategies, the document emphasizes that agriculture has a vital place in the economic development of the country as it contributes 29.4 per cent of GDP and employs about 64 per cent of the workforce. There has been a significant improvement in agricultural productivity which has helped in reducing rural poverty. It is noted that capital formation (at 1980-81 prices) in agriculture grew at tha rate of 6.05 per cent during 1989-90 to 1994-95. In the accelerated growth scenario for the Ninth Plan, efforts will need to be made to achieve an agricultural growth rate of 4.5 per cent per annum in contrast with 3.5 per cent growth rate during the Eighth Plan period on an average.

The role of basic inputs in agriculture cannot be underestimated. Timely and adequate availabilty of inputs for agriculture and agriculture-related infrastructure will need to receive special attention. Therefore, regional programmes have to be formulated in such a manner as to ensure provision of inputs to the farmer, particularly in the remote, hilly, backward and tribal areas. Likewise, augmentation of irrigation facilities is necessary to increase the gross cropped areas even under rainfed vonditions and invreasing cropping intensity in agriculture areas and assinging priority ot the completion of ongoing projects—both major and minor irrigation.

Ensuring Credit Flow: Another vital input is rural credit. Greater credit flow will be ensured to meet the investment requirements of the farming community for stepping up the growth of production. The approach paper of the Plan stresses that efforts would be made to ensure timely and adequate availability of credit, particularly to small and marginal farmers and tribal farmers at reasonable rates so as to enable them to make investments necessary for higher production. More importantly, the crop insurance scheme is going to receive a big thrust for providing security to marginal and small farmers in rainfed areas during the Ninth Plan period.

Poverty Estimates : Referring to the controversy over poverty estimates exercise, Prof. Dandavate points out that a group in the Plan panes has smoothed out some 'kinks' in the poverty estimate arising out of the appliation of the Lakadwala Committee methodology. He said that the group has suggested that in assessing rural poverty, the agricultural labourers' consumer price index should be used and for estimating urban poverty, the industrial workers' consumer price index should be untilized for updating the poverty line. It is hoped that the Planning Commission would finally decide on this issue during the final draft of the Plan.

Ninth plan approach

The main thrust of the Ninth Plan has been to evolve a shared vision of and a shared commitment to the national objectives and the development strategy not only in the government at all levels but also among all other economic agents. No development strategy can be successful unless each component of the economy works towards a common goal and purpose with the full realisation of the role that has to be played within an overall structure of responsibilities. Some of the tasks needed in respect of rural development are given below:

— The principal task during the Ninth Plan, therefore, is to build on the Eighth Plan, while tackling the problems that have emerged, particularly in areas such as capital formation in agriculture, social sector, regional disparity, and fiscal deficits. Indian economy is still vulnerable and the operation of a more open economic system has to be tempered by judicious public interventions to ensure that these vulnerabilities are gradually overcome.

— Since the planning is done for the entire nation, the strategies for resource augmentation need to cover not only the government at all levels but also those which would be available to other sections of the people.

— Since not all parts of the country are equally endowed to take advantage of growth opportunities, planned intervention is needed to ensure that large imbalances do not occur .

— The Indian economy still has a large number of its citizens who live in acute poverty both in rural and urban areas. Special employment programmes targeted to these people will continue in the Ninth Plan. Special attention will need to be paid to unorganized labour, particularly the agricultural landless labourer.

— There exist large disparities across the various social groups. The disadvantaged groups include members belonging to Scheduled Castes and Scheduled Tribes, other backward classes and minorities. In addition, women and children and the physically handicapped and disabled are also vulnerable. For these sections of society State intervention is required in order to provide them with adequate opportunities for education and employment in an attempt to involve them productively in the development process.

— It is heartening to note that the Plan has identified people's initiative and participation as a "key element" in the process of development, particularly in improving the effectiveness of development outlays which has been declining over the years. It has also recognized that the role of the government should be to facilitate the process of people's involvement by creating the right type of institutional infrastructure, particularly in rural areas.

The progress on this front so far has not been entirely satisfactory primarily due to the fact that the other tiers of the government were not fully integrated into the development strategy. The Plan also asserts that the process of social mobilization and development of people's initiatives cannot be achieved without the active support and involvement of the political system at all levels. In the Plan, the Panchayati Raj bodies in rural areas will be directly involved in the development process. People's involvement via their elected representatives will be realized through "democratic—decentralization".

— Co-operatives will be rejuvenated to enlist people's active participation in these societies. They will be liberated from tight bureaucratic control. Self-help groups, associations of workers or small producers, etc are other forms of institutions which will be encouraged to actively involve people in planning process and implementation. Government will seek active "partnership" with the voluntary sector in organizing and promoting these institutions.

— Domestic entrepreneurship, which is the backbone of the development process, will be fully encouraged through measures to enhance their competitive strength and to facilitate their growth and efficiency. In particular, the small-scale and village and home industries will be provided the proper environment for growth and diversification.

— While new initiatives are being taken for additional investment, optimum utilization of the existing infrastructure should not be neglected. This needs to be done by technology upgradation, systems improvement and ensuring public utilities function on commercial lines. Most importantly, care should be taken to ensure that in the provision of these services, the rural areas are provided their due share both in terms of magnitude as well as technology suited to their needs.

— In regard to subsidies, emphasis is laid to move to a system of transparent subsidies directed towards specific target-groups in a selective manner.

— The Indian Planning process had always laid emphasis on measures to ensure sustainability of the development process not only in economic terms, but also in terms of social and environmental factors. The Ninth Plan will carry this tradition further and consolidate on the creation of conditions for sustainable development.

Plan formulation–more freedom to States: The first novelty of the Ninth Plan is that the Planning Commission has decided to give more freedom to the State governments in formulating their plans. The Planning Commission has decided that in consultation with the Union Ministry of Finance, it will indicate the probable amount of Central assistance available to each State and the State governments would be left free to determine the size of their plans.

It may be recalled in this context that the earlier practice followed was that the State governments would propose specific size of the States' annual plans. The Planning Commission would scrutinize them in detail and then extract a promise of additional resource mobilization from the States before approving the plan size.

This gave unnecessary credibility to the size of the States' plans. Every state would push the plan size to unrealistically high level hoping that the Planning Commission would provide additional plan assistance. This never happened.

As a result, many States used to reduce their plans by December each year and wide gaps used to emerge between the original plan size and the final actual plan. What is more, the plan size came to be politicized at the State level. Nobody would accept the size of the plan lesser than the previous years' and it had to be necessarily higher at least by 10 per cent.

This kind of politicisation has been removed during the Ninth Five Year Plan period. The Planning Commission indicates the gross and net plan assistance available to each State and leaves the final size of the plan to be determined by the State government depending upon its capacity to raise additional revenue. This is the first change in the process of planning introduced by the Planning Commission during the Ninth Five Year Plan period.

Change in accounting format: The second change is that while determining the Central assistance to the State plans, the financial resources which used to flow from the financial institutions like LIC/NABARD/IDB/GIC plus statutory liquidity ratio (SLR) market borrowings were treated as Central government transfers. Though the Central government has control over the borrowing powers of the State governments, particularly when they are indebted to the Central government, these sources of funds are the prerogative of the State governments.

The State governments are free to raise funds through banks and other financial institutions depending upon the financial viability of the projects and their capacity to service the debt. However the Planning Commission and the Union Ministry of Finance have evolved a unified borrowing policy to protect the interests of poorer States and minimise the adverse impact of public borrowing on the economy. Therefore, these financial institutions were asked to co-ordinate their direct lending to the State governments. In this ways, the Planning Commission used to treat SLR and other such borrowings from the developmental financial institutions as part of Central assistance.

This practice was disliked by States like West Bengal an, therefore, the Planning Commission has now changed the accounting format in such a way as to show institutional finance and SLR borrowing as States' own resources available for plan purpose. This does not change the resource position of the States in any way. But it goes a long way in giving them and they need not be at the mercy of the Central government to raise funds from lending institutions.

Planning process decentralized: Thirdly, for the first time the approach paper recognized the federal nature of the Indian planning system and has devoted a separate chapter explaining how the Planning Commission is going to decentralize not merely plan formaulation but also the entire planning process including monitoring of implementation.

The document recognizes the implications of the far-reaching political change that has taken place in India. From the inception of the planning regime, the Central government used to be formed by a national party which used to dictate terms to the state governments But in the 1996 elections, no national party secured a majority and a number of regional parties have joined hands to form the United Front government at the Centre.

This is an unprecedented change in the political scenario. Consequently, the Planning Commision's thinking had to reflect this changed situation and give more voice to the State governments in the planning process. At the same time, the State governments are made to realize that they have to mobilize adequate additional resources and harmonize their budgets with a view to reducing fiscal imbalance in the economy.

Promoting federalism: Furthermore, the Planning Commission has been persuading the Central ministries to transfer a large number of Centrally-sponsored schemes (CSS) along with the corresponding funds to the State governments so that the Central domination in the development process and priorities of the States is reduced.

For instance, about 1823 Centrally-sponsored schemes with an outlay of Rs. 16,038. 19 crore were being implemented during the Eighth Plan period. The Chief Minister's conference held in July, 1996 expressed the view that the number of CSS should be reduced and transferred to the States. But the Central ministers are reluctant to transfer many schemes. They agreed to transfer the schemes worth Rs. 1,300 crore only.

Therefore, the Planning Commission has taken the initiative and is persuading the Central ministries to transfer more schemes along with the funds to the State governments as per the decision of the NDC which has laid down that CSS outlay sould not exceed one-sixth of total Central assistance.

In 1979-80, 71 CSS were transferred to the states with an outlay of Rs. 2,000 crore. While this is not a new phenomenon as it was done earlier also, it still augurs well for the States autonomy. The only occasion when it was done on a large scale was during the Janata Party rule which again gave prominence to true federal structure in the planning process.

The reconstituted Planning Commission believes that the principal task of planning in the post-reform era in our federal framework is to evolve a shared vision of and a shared commitment to the national objectives and the development strategy not only in the government at all levels but also among all economic agents.

The principal objective of the Ninth Plan is to build on the succsses of the VIII Plan, whike tackling the problems that have emerged, particularly in agriculture, living standard of the poor, infrastructure, social sector, regional disparity and fiscal deficits. The IX Plan will facilitate broadening and deepening the economic reforms process to ensure that the fruits of development reach the backward regions of the country and benefit the poorer sections of the society in a time-bound manner.

Provision of BMSs: The conference of State Chief Ministers held in july 1996 made a commitment to provide seven basic minimum services universally by AD 2000. They are (i) safe drinking water, (ii) access to primary health care, (iii) universal primary education, (iv) public housing assistance for the homeless, (v) extension of the midday meal scheme, (vi) road connectivity to all villages, and (vii) food security through the public distribution system for all families below the poverty line. The IX Plan will attempt to operationalize this commitment. The approach to the IX Plan outlines a long-term fiscal policy stance indicating methods by which resources of the governments at all levels can be augmented in order to reduce and eventually eliminate the revenue deficit at all levels. Along with aggregate economic growth, balanced regional development has been an essential component of our development strategy from the inception of planning. since not all regions of the country are well-endowed or equipped to take advantage of the growth objectives provided by the market, planned intervention continues to be essential to ensure reduction in regional imbalances.

Care for the poor: Our society continues to have a sizeable number of members who still suffer from abject poverty and deprivation. A vast majority of them do not get an opportunity to participate in the market economy.

They are neither able to contribute nor receive anytying from the market process. Appropriate public policies including skill-endowment to the market economy will be part of the Plan. Increasing the welfare of the socially and ecnonmically disadvantaged groups, including the Scheduled Castes, Scheduled Tribes and backward classes as well as minorities, handicapped and disabled and women and children is another objective of the Ninth Plan.

18

Indian Constitution and Institution Building

The Indian Constitution is a remarkable document as it strikes a balance between tradition and modernity, between a federal structure and a strong centre and between the demands of social justice and the rights of the individual. However, as we enter the 50th year of our Independence, perhaps it would be desirable to take a close second look at the Constitution with a view to removing possible distortions and streamlining its functioning. Democracy is often described as government of the people, by the people and for the people.

The Constitution, written as in the United States and other countries or unwritten but dependent on tradition as in the United Kingdom, lays down the framework for this form of government. But written or unwritten, there is a remarkable similarity between the two. In the United Kingdom the centre of power shifted first from the Crown to the nobles and then to the House of Commons. In the United States, judicial pronouncements have changed the complexion of the government. The federal Government has far more powers than was envisaged at first.

India became independent on August 15, 1947 and the Founding Fathers worked post haste to give the nation a new Constitution. The constitution was adopted by the Constitutent Assembly on November 26, 1949 and came into force on January 26, 1950. It was a remarkable achievement because many countries which became independent along with India were still floundering and trying to find their way in framing the Constitution. Countries, which became independent later, were looking at India's efforts. The Indian Constitution is a remarkable document as it strikes a balance between tradition and modernity, between a federal structure and strong centre between the demands of social justice and the rights of the individual and between conflicting demands in other areas.

Though the Founding Fathers were proud of the Constitution they had framed, they were also aware of their own limitations. As people move into a new house, they notice defects which had escaped the architect. Also conditions change and needs grow. Similarly, defects come to light as a Constitution comes into operation. Changes therefore become necessary and have to be made quickly and easily. As Dr. B.R. Ambedkar, the Law Minister, said on the day the Constitution was adopted, "The Assembly has not only refrained from putting a seal of finality and infallibility upon the Constitution by denying the people the right to amend the Constitution or making the amendment of the Constitution subject to the fulfilment of extraordinary terms and conditions, as in America or in Australia but has provided a more facile procedure foramending the Constitution". The President of the Constituent Assembly Dr. Rajendra Prasad observed "another important feature of the Constitution is that it enables amendments to be made without much difficulty".

Prime Minister Jawaharlal Nehru was even more forthright. Speaking on the first amendment made in 1951 he said, "People must realise that this great

Constitution of ours, which we laboured for so long, is not a final or rigid thing which must either be accepted or broken. A Constitution which is responsive to their ideas, in that it can be revised here and there, they will respect it all the more and they will not fight against it. Otherwise if you make them feel that it is unchangeable and cannot be touched the only thing that can be done by people who wish to change it, is to try and break it. That is a dangerous thing and a bad thing. Therefore it is a desirable and a good thing for people to realise that this very fine Constitution which we have fashioned is good in so far as it goes but as society changes, as conditions change, we mend it in the proper way".

The members of the Constituent Assembly were conscious that they had been elected by members ofthe Provincial Assemblies who had themselves been elected on a limited franchise. How could they put restrictions on the House of the People which was to be set up on the principle of universal adult franchise ? The leaders were also aware that in the years to come, conditions would change, new demands would be made and met and it would be the duty of the new rulers to meet the challenges as they came up. It was therefore that they left the way open for easy amendments without going through the arduous process of forming a new Constituent Assembly.

Events proved that the Founding Fathers of the Constitution showed robust common sense when they decided that the process of amending the Constitution should be easy. The first amendment was made in 1951 to make it possible among other things to carry out land reforms and abolish the zamindaris. Also, it was decided that reasonable restrictions could be placed on the exercise of Fundamental Rights in the interests of society. Since then, the Constitution has been amended more than 75 times. Most of these amendments were made to remove difficulties in the working of the Constitution, but others like the one about Panchayati Raj and Municipalities gave an entirely new dimension to administration by devolution of powers to local self-government bodies. The amendment about reservation for women in legislative bodies will add one more dimension to the Constitution.

The result is that the Constitution today resembles an ancient edifice to which additions and modifications have been made from time to time to suit the needs but in the process, the character of the original structure has been changed beyond recognition. Some of the provisions of the Constitution like introducing prohibition or banning cow slaughter have been found to be impossible to implement. Others like drafting a Common Civil Code have met with stiff opposition form sections of society. Similarly many of the Directive Principles of State Policy have been reduced to mere expression of pious intentions.

The Constituent Assembly utilised the period between August 15, 1947 and November 26, 1949 to draft the Constitution which came into force on January 26, 1950. On August 15 1997 India completes fifty years of Independence. It will be in the fitness of things if the task of taking a second look at the Constitution is attempted so as to remove the cobwebs and to streamline the working. A Committee of Parliament can undertake the job with inputs from politicians, experts in constitutional law, academics and journalists. The changes can be made by the time the nation celebrates the 50th anniversary of the enforcement of the Constitution and the establishment of the Indian Republic.

The paths to peace and freedom and equal rights were strewn with thorns and hurdles were placed at all steps. the White rule became a blot on the world conscience. Denial to right to live brought an upsurge among the Black South Africans. In their struggle, they found India and the Indians settled there as a great source of inspiration. It was not because Mahatma Gandhi's association with South Africa in the initial years of his political life that made India so receptive to the aspirations of the Black South Africans.

Perhaps in the South African freedom movement and struggle for equality was seen the same psyche of the Indian people who suffered humiliation, imprisonment and torture in India during the long independence struggle. Indians felt genuinely for the Black South Africans. So did the goverment.

In less than a decade's existence as an independent nation, India brought before the world a new concept of governance based on the principle of "Panchsheel". It was but natural for a country that has a long tradition of tolerance. India with numerous languages and multiplicity of religion itself symbolises co-existence. Mutual respect for each other, irrespective of differences, demonstrates Indian ethos.

It is in this context, the Bandung conference in April 1955 that adopted "Panchsheel" created a new concept for the world already handed over to violence and turmoil. The Bandung conference had five proponents: India, Indonesia, Burma, Sri Lanka and Pakistan. The Bandung conference was preceded by the bombing of the Air India plane carrying delegates and journalists over South China sea. Evidently, forces that wanted the settlement of disputes through terrorism asserted their right to show their way of solving issue and problems.

INDIA, a Union of States, as a Sovereign Socialist Secular Democratic Republic with a parliamentary system of government. The Republic is governed in terms of the Constitution, which was adopted by Constituent

Assembly on 26 November, 1949 and came into force on 26 January, 1950.

The Constitution which evisages parliamentary from of government is federal in structure with unitary features. President of India is constitutional head of executive of the Union. Article 74(1) of the Constitution provides that there shall be a Council of Ministers with the Prime Minister as head to aid and advise president who shall, in exercise of his functions, act in accordance with such advice. Real executive power thus vests in Council of Ministers with Prime minister as head. Council of Ministers is collectively responsible to the House of the People (Lok Sabha). Similarly, ini states, Governor is head of executive, but it is the Council of Ministers with Chief Minister as head in whom real executive power vests. Council of Ministers of a state is collectively responsible to Legislative Assembly.

The Constitution distributes legislative power between Parliament and state legislatures and provides for vesting of residual powers in Parliament. Power to amend the Constitution also vests in Parliament. The Constitution has provision for independence of judiciary, Comptroller and Auditor-General, Public service commmissions and Chief Election Commissioner.

India comprises 25 states and seven union territories. States are: Andhra Pradesh, Assam, Arunachal Pradesh, Bihar, Goa, Gujraat, Haryana, himachal Pradesh, Jammu and Kashmir, Karnataka, Kerala, Madhya Pradesh, Maharashtra, Manipur, Megthalaya, Mizoram, Nagaland, Orissa, Punjab, Rajasthan, Sikkim, Tamil Nadu, Tripura, Uttar Pradesh and West Bengal. Union territories are: Andaman and Nicobar Islands, Chandigarh, Dadra and Nagar Haveli, Daman and Diu, Delhi, Lakshadweep and Pondicherry.

The Constitution of India provides for a single and uniform citizenship for whole of India. Every person who was at commencement of the Constitution (26 January 1950) domiciled in the territory of India and: (a) who was born in the territory of India or (b) either of whose parents was born in the territory of India or (c) who has been ordinarily resident in the territory of India for not less than five years immediately preceding such commencement, shall be a citizen of India. The Citizenship Act, 1955 provides for acquisition and termination of citizenship after the commencement of the Constitution.

The Constitution offers all citizens, individually and collectively, some basic freedoms. These are guaranteed in the Constitution in the form of six broad categories of Fundamental Rights which are justiceable. Article 12 to 35 contained in Part III of the Constitution deal with Fundamental Rights. These are: (i) right to equality including equality before law, prohibition of discrimination on grounds of religion, race, caste, sex or place of birth and equality of opportunity in matters of employment; (ii) right to freedom of speech and expression; assembly; association or union; movement; residence; and right to practice any profession or occupation (some of these rights are subject to security of the State, friendly relations with foreign countries, public order, decency or morality); (iii) right against exploitation, prohibiting all forms of forced labour, child labour and traffic in human beings; (iv) right to freedom of conscience and free profession, practice and propagation of religion; (v) right of any section of citizens to conserve their culture, language or script and right of minorities to establish and administer educational institutions of their choice, and (vi) right to constitutional remedies for enforcement of Fundamental Rights.

By the 42nd Amendment of the Constitution, adopted in 1976, Fundamental Duties of the citizens have also been enumerated. Article 51 'A' contained in Part IV A of the Constitution deals with Fundamental Duties. These enjoin upon a citizen among other things, to abide by the Constitution, to cherish and follow noble ideals which inspired our national struggle for freedom, to defend the country and render national service when called upon to do so and to promote harmony and spirit of common brotherhood amongst all people of India transcending religious, linguistic and regional or sectional diversities.

The Constitution lays down certain Directive Principles of State Policy which though not justiceable, are 'fundamental in governance of the country' and it is 'the duty of the State to apply these principles in making laws'. These lay down that the State shall strive to promote welfare of people by securing and protecting as effectively as it may a social order in which justice–social, economic and political, shall inform all institutions of national life. The State shall direct its policy in such a manner as to secure the right of all men and women to an adequate means of livelihood, equal pay for equal work and within limits of its economic capacity and development, to make effective provision for securing the right to work, education and to public assistance in the event of unemployment, old age, sickness and disablement or other cases of undeserved want. The State shall also endeavour to secure to workers a living wage, humane conditions of work, a decent standard of life and full involvement of workers in management of industries.

In economic sphere, the State is to direct its policy in such a manner as to secure distribution of ownership and control of material resources of community to subserve the common good and to ensure that operation of economic system does not result in concentration of wealth and means of production to common detriment.

Some of the other important directives relate to provisions of opportunities and facilities for children to develop in a healthy manner, free and compulsory education for all children up to the age of 14; promotion of educational and economic interests of scheduled castes, scheduled tribes and other weaker sections; organisation of village panchayats; separation of judiciary from executive, promulgation of a uniform civil code for whole country; protection of national monuments; promotion of justice on a basis of equal opportunity; provision of free legal aid; protection and improvement of environment and safeguarding of forests and wildlife of the country and promotion of international peace and security, just and honourable relations between nations, respect for international law, treaty obligations and settlement of international disputes by arbitration.

Politicians will try to shy away from the task on the ground that it will mean opening a Pandora's box, which it will certainly be. The States will demand more powers even autonomy, while some will ask for more powers for the centre. Conflicting claims and demands will be made. Should we have directive Principles of State Policy which cannot be enforced in a Court of Law? All these and more will have to be looked into.

But there are some problems which cannot be pushed under the carpet any more. When the Constitution was framed, the Assembly had to a large extent placed before itself the Westminster form of Government. In such a form of government, two political parties vie for power. There is a general agreement on basic problems and policies. The Founding Fathers had possibly hoped that in course of time in India also, two rival parties would emerge. But this has not happened.

We have a plethora of political parties. Three successive elections to the Lok Sabha did not give any political party a clear majority. Even when a politial party has the majority, its leader is always worried about keeping his flock together. Policies are often framed not so much for national good but for narrow political ends.

But what is the remedy if the electorate does not give a clear verdict in election after electon? The Constitution has no provision for direct rule by the President at the Centre because this might result insubversion of democracy and the establishment of a dictatorship. At the State level, the Constitution provides for imposition of President's rule. Dr. Ambedkar had expressed the hope that his provision might never be used. Events have proved otherwise and in the last 47 years, it has been used more than 100 times. There is justification for doing so when separatist forces and militancy pose threat to democracy as in Punjab, Jammu & Kashmir and Assam but no justificaton when it is used for political purposes.

But what is the way out at the Centre or in the States if no party gets a clear majority in election after election? A poor country can ill afford the luxury of election after election without a verdict in favour of any single party. Students and scholars of political science and leaders of political parties have been worried about this for a long time. Even during the days of Mrs. Indira Gandhi a suggestion was made that India should go in for a presidential form of government. The former Union Minister and senior parliamentarian Mr. Vasant Sathe has long been advocating this and has also said that this change can be made with a few changes in the Constitution.

There is another area where the distortion is worsening every day. Under the original scheme of things, a population of 7½ lakh elected a member of the Lok Sabha. The first Lok Sabha thus had 489 elected members. The Constitution also provided that the number of seats would go up according to the figures of population in the previous census. The seats went up to 545 by 1976. But it was felt that the increase gave an unfair advantage to the States which did not take up the family planning programme in earnest. Therefore, the number of seats in the Lok Sabha and in the Assemblies was frozen at the figures of 1976. By an amendment of the Constitution it was decided that the readjustment ofseats on the basis of population would be made only after the figures of the first census after the year 2000 were publidhed. The next Lok Sabha election would be held in 2001 which is also the year in which the next census will be held. By then the figures of the census are not likely to be available. But a serious thought will have to be given now to the question of the ratio between the population and the number of seats in the Lok Sabha and the State Assemblies. If the original scheme of one Lok Sabha member for every 7.50 lakh population were to be followed the Lok Sabha todays should have a membership of more than 1300. By the turn of the century the population of India is likely to go up to 100 crore and the membership of the Lok Sabha would have to be more than 1400. The Uttar pradesh Assembly would similiarly have a strength of 800 today. It will be impossible to manage such a large House.

But then if this is not done, the Lok Sabha constituencies would be so large in terms of population that it will be impossible for a candidate to contact the voters and for a candidate to contact the voters and for the M.P. to maintain contacts with his constituency. Outer Delhi today has electorate of nearly 30 lakh. Thane in Maharashtra comes a close second with an electorate of 26 lakh. It is well nigh impossible for anyone to claim that he can look after the interests of such a large electorate much less to visit the distant areas regularly. Many constituencies of the U.P. Assembly today have the same electorate as the Lok Sabha had in 1952. A fresh delimitation can only solve the problem partially. What is needed is a fresh look and a new initiative.

Under the present system the candidate who gets the largest number of votes is declared elected. Frequently the combined votes of the other candidates are more than his votes. It has also happened that a political party might get a majority of the seats. A swing of a mere 5 per cent can make a tremendous difference. Any review of the Constitution must look at this anomaly and find ways to remove it.

The Union executive consists of President, Vice President and Council of Ministers with Prime Minister at the head to aid and advice President.

President is elected by members of an electoral college consisting of elected members of both House of Parliament and Legislative Assumblies of the states in accordance with the system of proportional representation by means of single transferable vote. To secure uniformity among states inter se as well as parity between the states, as a whole, and the Union, suitable weightage is given to each vote. President must be a citizen of India, not less than 35 years of age and qualified for election as member of the Lok Sabha. His term of office is five years and he is eligible for re-election. His removal from office is to be in accordance with procedure prescribed in Article 61 of the Constitution. (He may, by writing under his hand addressed to Vice President, resign his office.)

Executive power of the Union is vested in President and is exercised by him either directly or through officers subordinate to him in accordance with the Constitution.

Supreme Command of defence forces of the Union also vests in him. President summons, prorogues, addresses, sends messages to Parliament and dissolves the Lok Sabha; promulgates Ordinances at any time, except when both Houses of Parliament are in session; makes recommendations for introducing financial and money bills and gives assent to bills; grants pardons, reprieves, respites or remissions of punishment or suspends, remits or commutes sentences in certain cases. When there is a failure of the constitutional machinery in a state, he can assume to hmself all or any of the functions of the government of that state. President can proclaim emergency in the country if he is satisfied that a grave emergency exists whereby security of India or any part of its territory is threatened whether by war or external aggression or armed rebellion.

Vice President is elected by members of an electoral college consisting of members of both Houses of Parliament in accordance with the system of proportional representation by means of single transferable vote. He must be a citizen of India, not less than 35 years of age and eligible for election as a member of the Rajya Sabha. His term of office is five years and he is eligible for re-election. His removal from office is to be in accordance with procudure prescribed in Article 67 b.

Vice Presidents is ex-offico Chairman of the Rajya Sabha and acts as President when the latter is unable to discharge his functions due to absence, illness or any other cause or till the election of a new President (to be held within six months) when a vacancy is caused by death, resignation or removal or otherwise of President. While so acting, he ceases to perform the function of the Chairman of the Rajya Sabha.

There is a Council of Ministers headed by PrimeMinister to aid and advise President in exercise of his functions. Prime Minister is appointed by President who also appoints other ministers on the advice of Prime Minister. The Council is collectively responsible to the Lok Sabha. It is the duty of the Prime Minister to communicate to President all decisions of Council of Ministers relating to administeration of affairs of the Union and proposals for legislation and information relating to them.

The Council of Ministers comprises Ministers who members of Cabinet, Ministers of·State (independent charge), Ministers of State and Deputy Ministers.

Legislature of the Union which is called Parliament, consists of President and two Houses, known as Council of States (Rajya Sabha) and House of the People (Lok Sabha). Each House of Parliament has to meet within six months of its previous sitting. A joint sitting of two Houses can be held in certain cases.

A switch over to the Presidential Form of Government will be a far reaching change which can only be made after a nation wide debate. But the immediate problems of the electoral system need to be examined quickly. A 'hung' Lok Sabha or State Assembly leads to defections and politics of expendiency and negates democracy. We have to find an answer to it. Introduction of proportional representation is not prctical in a large country like India. But should we then have a system of direct election for half the seats and proportional representation for the other half? This experiment has been tried succesfully in Japan.

Another area for attention is the role of the Rajya Sabha and the Legislative Councils in some States. These were envisaged as chambers of revision but over the years have largely become chambers where the work is mostly duplicated. Our Rajya Sabha is neither as powerful as the Senate in the USA nor powerless as the

House of Lords in the U.K. Its powers and functioning deserve a close second look. Unlike the Lok Sabha, the Rajya Sabha is supposed to represent the States. It has therefore been laid down that its members should be normally resident in the State from which they are elected. But more and more instances come up where he does not live. It is easy to look at this as a technical violation of the Constitution. But another aspect is often overlooked. States like Punjab and Jammu & Kashmir were for long years been under President's rule and the Legislative Assemblies had been dissolved and could not elect members to the Rajya Sabha, elections to the Lok Sabha were also not held there. Should the people of these States be denied the right of representation at both the Central and State levels for no fault of their own? Election tot he Rajya Sabha from another state might not be strictly according to the letter of the Constitution but it at least gives a politician from such a State to put forward the views of the people and to air their grievances.

It is well known that militancy in Punjab was limited to a few districts and in Jammu & Kashmir to the Kashmir Valley. But since the Assembly had been dissolved and the State placed under Central rule, areas where there was comparative peace could also not go to the polls even for the Lok Sabha. They were penalised for no faults of theirs. Any review of the Constitution has to consider this question and find a solution.

It is to the credit of India that while other countries which became independent along with her have had long periods of dictatorship or military rule, democracy has continued to grow in India. The Indian voter has been no respecter of men and has not hesitated to throw out powerful leaders if he found that they were not performing well. The base has widened with the devolution of powers to the local self-governing bodies.

The proposal to reserve seats for women in legislative bodies is proof of the fact that political parties forget their differences on giving greater powers to the neglected segments of society. Changes have been made in the Constitution to keep pace with the times.

As India enters the 50th year of her Independence it is time to do a soul searching and to examine whether the Constitution needs a close second look so as to remove the cobwebs and to remove the distortions and discrepancies.

The Indian Armed Forces have many outstanding achievements to their credit. However, as war or any external threat requires total mobilisation in a democracy, maximum transparency alone can ensure cooperation on the part of the people in all respects. Independent India was born in the midst of hostilities in Jammu and Kashmir. The holocaust that followed the partition of the country, the migration of people and the sudden attack by pakistan in Kashmir valley in October, 1947 created a feeling of insecurity among the people. The armed forces left behind by the Britishers and the infrastructure then available however proved adequate enough to repulse the Pakistani mischief.

Subsequently, the easy manner in which we secured the integration of Junagarh (1947), Hyderabad (1948) and Goa (1961) brought in an element of overconfidence. Truely speaking, we were lost in an attitude of complacency believing in the good intentions of our neighbours, particularly China.

The rude shock delivered by China in Oct., 1962 made the leaders at the helm of affiars realise the need for an all weather Army, Navy and Air Force. Fear and insecurity had then gripped the people and some had even doubted our capability to protect the territorial integrity of the country. People in the North-East, for a moment, felt they were left to fend for themselves. In the background of these developments, one can say that planning for defence preparedness had its beginning after the humiliating Chinese invasion in the North-East.

Thanks to the assistance extended by the then Soviet Union in the development of our Air Force, Navy and Army, besides the help provided by the United Kingdom and France for expansion and modernisation of sea and air elements, we were able to check a renewed Pakistani onslaught in Jammu and Kashmir and Rann of Kutch in Gujarat in 1665. Pakistan was well and truely beaten and the Tashkent Peace Accord held good till 1971.

Meanwhile, all the three defence services were gradually building up their strength in terms of armour, aircraft carrier, submarines and air defence fighters. Thus when in 1971, after Sheikh Mujibur Rehman gave a call for a mass freedom struggle on March, 26 in Dacca, the Indian armed forces were definitely in a position of superiority to take on the challenge to protect millions of refugees as well as the borders.

During the last 25 years, defence preparedness, as linked to Policy Planning, has been on an ad-hoc basis, if not in fits and starts. No doubt, there has been the acquisition of the T-72M tanks and the BMP series covering the Infantry Combat Vehicle and the Bofors 155 MM field howitzers. The Navy has gained in the acquisition of the Kilo class submarines, the aircraft carrier Viraat and the West German Hunter Killer class submarines.

The Air force has been steadily strengthened with the induction of the Jaguars, MIG-21, MIG-25, MIG-23, 27 and 29. The Mirage 2000, the AN-32 and the IL-76 long haul transports have also added punch to the Air Force. But this by no means reflects a long—term defence policy planning since all these acquisitions virtually came long after the requirements were made known, resulting in heavy cost escalations.

And some of them were clouded in controversies. As a result of which for nearly a despite urgent needs being repeatedly highlighted by the Armed Forces.

At the Army Headquarters in New Delhi, the Chief of the Army Staff is assisted by the Vice-Chief of the Army Staff and seven other Principal Staff Officers, namely, two Deputy Chiefs of the Army Staff, Adjtant General, Quarter-Master General, Master General of Ordnance, Military Secretary and Engineer-in-Chief.

The Army is organised into five operational Commands, viz., Southern, Eastern, Western, Central and Northern Command and one Training Command. Each Command is under a General Officer Commanding-in-Chief who holds the rank of Lieutenant General. General Officer Commanding-in-Chief commanding an operative command is the commander of demarcated geographical area and has both field and static formations under the command. The major field formations are Corps, Division and Brigade, commanded by a General Officer Commanding of the rank of Major General and Brigadier, respectively. The major static formations are Areas, independent Sub-Areas and Sub-Areas. An Area is commanded by a General Officer Commanding of the rank of Major General and an independent Sub-Area and Sub-Area by a Brigadier.

The Army consists of a number of arms and services. These are: Armoured Corps, Regiment of Artillery, Corps of Air Defence Artillery, Army Aviation Corps, Corps of Engineers, Corps of Signals, Mechanised Infantry, Infantry, Army Service Corps, Army Ordnance Corps, Corps of Electrical and Mechanical Engineers, Remount and Veterinary Corps, Military Police, Judge Advocate General Department, Army Physical Training

Corps, Poineer Corps, Army Postal Service, Territorial Army, Defence Security Corps. In addition, the Army has its own Recruiting Organisation, Record Offices, Depots, Boys Establishments and Selection Centres and Training institutions.

The Navy responsible for defence and security of India's maritime interests and assests, both in times of war and peace. The Chief of the Naval Staff at the Naval Headquarters, New Delhi, is assisted by four Principal Staff Officers, namely, the Vice Chief of Naval Staff, the Deputy Chief of Naval Staff, Chief of Personnel and Chief of Material.

The Navy has three commands i.e., Western, Eastern and Southern with their headquarters located at Bombay, Visakhapatnam and Cochin respectively. Each Command is headed by a Flag Officer Commanding-in-Chief in the rank of Vice Admiral. Western Command and Eastern Command have under them operational fleets i.e., Western and Eastern Fleets comprising warships, submarines, aircraft and other support ships. Southern Naval Command is responsible for all training activities of the Indian Navy.

The Indian Navy is a well balanced three dimensional force consisting of sophisticated missile capable warships, two aircraft carriers, minesweepers, advanced submarines and the latest aircraft in its inventory. Many of the warships are of indigenous design and have been constructed in Indian shipyards. These ships compare well with the ships of similar capability constructed by the advanced countries. The Naval forces are maintained and supported by modern dockyard facilities encompassing state-of-the art technology. At present, it has two major Naval bases at Bombay and Visakhapatnam.

The Coast Guard was constituted as an armed force of the Unin in 1978 under the Coast Guard Act, to protect the maritime and other national intersts in the maritime zones of India covering an area of approximately 28 lakh sq km. The force, which in headed by Director General Coast Guard is functioning under the effective control of the Ministry of Defence.

The headquarters of the force is presently located in New Dehli and regional headquaters are at Bombay, Mardras and Port Blair. The three regions, namely, Western, Eastern and Andaman and Nicobar cover 11 districts, one in each of the nine coastal states in the mainland and two in Andaman and Nicobar Islands. At present, the Coast Guard district headquarters are located at Porbandar in Gujarat, Bombay in Maharashtra, Vasco-da-Gama in Goa, New Mangalore in Karnataka and at Cochin in Kerala. Similary on the East coast, these are located at Madras in Tamil Nadu, Vizag in Andhra Pradesh, Paradeep in Orissa and Haldia in West Bengal. In addition independent Coast Guard stations are located at Vadinar, Okha, Tuticorin and Mandapam. Coast Guard air stations are in operation at Daman and Madras and Air Enclaves at Goa, Calcutta and Bombay. Establishment of stations at Kavaratti and Kamorta are being planned.

The force has effectively served national interests in high-risk areas. Foreign trawlers fishing illegally have been apprehended. Coast Guard ships and aircraft have been regularly assisting the customs authorities in anti-smuggling operations. Besides, the force is available for search and rescue operations, anti-pollution and other duties in the maritime zones of the country. The recent oil spill situations off Andaman and Nicobar and Goa were efficiently handled by the Coast Guard.

The Air Forse is organised both on functional as well as geographical basis. There are five operational commands. These are: Western Air Command, South-Western Air Command, Central Air Command, Eastern Air Command and Southern Air Command. In addition, Maintenance Command and Training Command are two functional commands.

At the Air Headquarters in New Delhi, the Chief of the Air Staff is assisted by the Vice-Chief of Air Staff, Deputy Chief of Air Staff, Air Officer Incharge Personnel, Air Officer Incharge Administration, Air Officer Incharge Maintenance and Inspector General (Flight Safety and Inspection). Each of these six Principal Staff Officers is assisted by an Assistant Chief of the Air Staff.

Today, the Air Force has an array of modern aircraft on its inventory besides other hi-tech electronic and support equipment. The aircraft fleet consists of fighter bombers, air superiority fighters, interceptors, transport and logistic aircraft and helicopters. The fighters force comprises MiG-21 variants, MiG-23s, MiG-25s, MiG-27s and Jaguars which represent the modern generation strike aircraft. Older generation aircraft like the Hunters and Canberras are presently used in training and ancillary roles. MiG-29s and Mirage-2000s are air defence aircraft of the present generation. The transport fleet consists of IL-76s, AN-32s, the indigenously produced HS-748s, Dornier-228 which are manufactured under licence by HAL and Boeing 737s which are used for VIP duties. While the IL-76s provides the Air Force with heavylift and strategic capabilities, AN-32s and HS-748s are also used in training role besides performing air maintenance and communication duties. The helicopter fleet consists of Chetak, Cheetah, MI-8, MI-17 and the heavy-lift MI-26 which is the largest helicopter in the world. All these aircraft are used for high altitude operations and provide logistics support to our ground forces. Chetak/Cheetah helicopters maufactured by HAL for the Air Force, are also used as Anti-Tank Guided Missile (ATGM) carriers, air borne Forward Air Controller (FAC) and for search and rescue operations. MI-8 helicopters are specially modified to undertake tasks in Antarctica. In addition, the force has been supplemented with MI-25 which performed yeoman service for the IPKF in Sri Lanka and MI-35 attack helicopters. HPT-32 and HJT-16 Kiran, both manufactured by HAL are used as basic and applied stage trainers respectively with the Kiran being supplemented by Polish Iskara aircraft. A landmark in the IAD was the commissioning of the first batch of women pilots on 17 December 1994. These pilots are now serving in front line transport Squadrons. The next batch women pilots is currently undergoing helicopter training and all have achieved solo flight status on Chetak and Cheetah helicopters.

As for the Army, the project plans centred around the 155 mm Bofors guns were completely neutralised for reasons well known. In the process the ambitious programme of manufacturing about 1000 field Howitzers aided by technology transfer from Sweden for manufacture of ammunition got stalled. Worse still the Army's urgent requirements of the self-propelled guns of the same calibre got stuck up.

In Spite of the tumult over its acquisition, the 400 odd Swedish Howitzers played a decisive role in both the north-west as well as the north-east borders. Pakistan's repeated attempts togain a foothold in the Siachen Glacier were foiled by the Army's timely deployment and effective use of the Bofors guns.

So too, in the eastern sector, the advent of the 155 mm guns and their potential for long range bombardment in the himalayan heights put the Chinese in check and there were no more intrusions like the one in Arunachal Pradesh in the late 80's.

It would not be out of place to mention that the Indian Army has been involved in the arduous task of neutralising insurgencies in the entire North-East during the last 50 years. Neighbouring countries like China, Burma and the then East Pakistan (Bangaldesh) evinced more than usual interest in provoking various insurgent and ethnic groups in a bid to destabilise the country and bleed our defence forces.

The Indian Army nonetheless tackled the situation with minimum force required and to a large extent has succeeded in winning the sympathy of the people through various aid to civilian population. More than two division of troops had to be deployed and kept on alert to foil underground insurgencies aided and abetted by hostile countries. In fact, this became part of our defence preparedness plans and specialised units and training centres had to be raised.

To relieve the troops from being locked in such insurgency situatons and policing roles, the Rashtriya Rifles has been established. Forty Batallions have now taken up positions in such conflict situations. The Army will concentrate on its primary role to keep fit and trained to face any eventuality from across the borders. In addition, the BSF and Assam Rifles are there to assist the armed forces.

Although the Navy has been slightly better off with its own naval design Bureau and a home shipping industry, the lack of funds has slowed down the pace of construction of new warships. On this score one cannot fault the Navy for lack of planning. It is more in the sphere of implementation. Yet both government and shipyards have to be congratulated for additions, especially in the field of Corvettes, Missile Boats and Submarine, two of which were built at Mazagon Docks, Bombay. There is an ongoing project for the construction of three destoyers of 6000 tonnes each beginning with the Delhi, Mysore and Mumbai. Three advanced and modified versions of the Godavari class are under construction at the Garden Reach Workshop, Calcutta and the first 'Brahmaputra' has already been launched.

The demand is there for more subs, both of the Kilo and the German Hunter class but government is yet to take a decisison. Fortunately the cash crunch has not affected the progressive addition of Sea Harriers with the Navy but they require an additional platform in time, since Vikrant has already been virtually decommissioned. The life of aircraft carier Viraat is also getting shorter by the Years. Fortunately, both the nodel Ministry and the Navy is in the process of acquiring a sea control ship, possibly from Russia. As a lông term option, India of course has the potential to build its own Aircraft Carrier at Cochin shipyard.

The Navy with its spreading blue water capability has no doubt created an impact on neighbouring countries, especially in the East and even caused a sense of alarm in far away Australia which has however with the passage of time been convinced that India has no expansionist intentions except to guard its coastline particularly its Exclusive Economic Zone and Oil Installations on the high seas.

The Indian Navy has also raised the 'Marine Commando Force', a specialised unit which can operate in various under water and off-shore areas. India is the second country after the USA to build up this highly mobile and potent naval commando force. During the operations in Sri Lanka, the Marine Commando Force won laurels and proved its worth as a deterrent to the enemy.

The maintsay of the Air Force has been the MIG fleet ranging from MIG-21 to MIG-29, supplemented by the Jaguars and the Mirage-2000. It goes the credit of the Air Force that it showed its capabilities in combined operations first in 1971 and some 20 years later in the Maldives. In 1971, the Air Force was ready to take on the task of dropping a para batallion over Tangail to deliver a deadly psychological blow that hastened the surrender of Pakistani forces in Bangaldesh. Such airborne operations had become imperative due to a threat posed by an American Carrier group heading towards Chittagong. It would not be out of place to mention that the press played the role of a force multiplier. A foreign news agency reported that a para brigade had been dropped on the outskirts of Dacca and that did the trick.

But more outstanding was the reflex action response of the Air Force in fulfilling the requirement of the maldives President Abdul Gayoom in meeting a coup attempt by foreign mercenaries against his democratically elected government. In less than six hours, the Air Force with its giant IL-76 had landed Indian troops in and around Male, the Maldivian Capital and foiled the coup attempt. In this operation, the Air Force displayed its combat and communication capabilities across the Indian ocean and this was indeed an eye opener for Western Powers. Not only this, it was a snub for Pakistan as its offer for help was rejected by the Maldivian President.

Fortunately, for the Air Force, it has also a large manufacturing and overhauling base with rich experience in the production and maintenance of almost the entire MIG fleet and Jaguars. It is against this background that these facilities will not only be upgraded but considerably augmented by the project for modernisation of the MIG-21 BIS fleet of 125 fighters. Two prototypes of the upgraded MIG-21 BIS are expected shortly and the HAL will undertake the fabrication of the updated versions. This programme is expected to be completed in less than two years and should amply make up for repeated delays in the LCA project. The air defence of the country would be well secured with the new look MIG-21 BIS fleet, which will be equipped with four times higher fire power against ground targets and would be an even match for F-16 in service with Pak Air Force.

The acquisition of the Sukhoi-30 culminates a long wait by the Air Force, which had spelt out its requirements for this multi-role air superiority fighter far back in 1990. For the first time perhaps India has gone for a new weapon system not merely based on the Pakistan syndrome but with much wider perspective that will cover portions of China, Myanmar and South-East Asia. In addition, the regional security requirements will be amply met by the longer range and sweep of the Sukhois which could neutralise any hostile activity emanating from countries in the neighbourhood like Iran, Afghanistan and even possibly Central Asian States. It will be pertinent to point out in this context that Sukhois will have mid air refuelling capability. India has signed a contract with Russia for 40 Sukhois and significantly this includes the transfer of technology and indigenous manufacture of this multi-role fighter planes. For the first time the Russion agencies have agreed to permit DRDO to participate in R & D and joint development of avoinics of the aircraft.

Defence Research and Development Organisation (DRDO) was established in 1958 by amalgamating Defence Science Organisation and some of the technical development establishments. A separate Department of Defence Research and Development was formed in 1980 which operates through network of 50 laboratories/ establishments. The Department is engaged in the pursuit of self-reliance in critical technologies of relevance to national security. It formulates and executes programmes of scientific research, design and development leading to induction of state-of-the-art weapons, platforms and other equipments required by the Armed Forces. It functions under the control of Scientific Adviser to Raksha Mantri who is also Secretary, Defence Research and Development.

Research and development activities of the Department cover important demarcated disciplines like aeronatuics, rockets and missiles, electronics and instrumentation, combat vehicles, engineering systems, naval systems, armament technology including explosives research, system sciences including advanced computing, high altitude agriculture, physiology, food technology, nuclear medicine and allied sciences. In addition, the Department also assists the Services by rendering technical advice regarding formulation of requirements, evaluation of systems to be acquired, fire and explosive safety and mathematical/statistical analysis of operational problems.

The notable development successes of the Department include flight stimulators for aircraft, light field gun, 5.56 mm rifle, charge line mine clearing system for safe passage of vehicles in the battlefield, illuminating ammunition for enhancing night fighting capabilities, cluster weapons system for fighter aircraft, naval mines and new generation bombs for high speed aircraft and low-level bombing. Different radars like low-level tracking radar Indra-I and Indra-II for Army and Air Force, light weight field artillery radar, battlefield surveillance radar, secondary surveillance radar hae been developed. Bridge Layer Tank-Kartik, military bridging system, advanced ship sonar systems, advance sonobuoy, naval decoys, naval simulators, torpedo launchers, advanced materials and composites for military applications are also some of the other achievements of the Department.

The main battle tank Arjun having superior fire power, high mobility and excellent protection has been successfully developed. Army has accepted the tank for induction in Service and the tank is now under troop trails in actual field conditions. Simultaneously, planning action has been initiated by Department of Defence Production and Supplies for productionisation of MBT Arjun. A Light Combat Aircraft (LCA) is under hardware fabrication and engineering stage and integration of some of the sub-assemblies has already commended. An advanced technology gas turbine engine GTX-35VS named Kaveri for use in LCA is under development under a separate programme. Integrated Guided Missile Development Programme (IGMDP) comprises four missile system, namely, Prithvi, surface-to-surface tactical battlefield missile; Akash, medium range surface-to-air missile; Trishul, short range surface-to-air missile; and Nag, third generation anti-tank missile. The programme also included development of a re-entry technology demonstrator project called Agni.

The other major programmes which are in advanced stage of development/productionisation are: Pilotless Target Aircraft (PTA), Composite Sonar and Tactical Weapon Control System-'Panchendriya' for Navy, LMG and carbine in 5.56 mm calibre and multi-barrel rocket launching system-'Pinaka'. A Marine Acoustic Research Ship-'Sagardhwani' has been designed and built indigenously. The ship is one of the most modern research. A PACE-PLUS parallel processing computer, configured with advanced commercially available micro-processors as computing nodes, has been designed and developed.

The Department has also rendered assistance to para-military and police agencies by way of supply of bullet proof vehicles, bullet proof vests, amenity vehicles, such as kitchen lorry, communication equipment, water pressure jet based anti-riot vehicles and several other types of equipments. The Department also offers specialised training at its two primier training institutions.

Following are the commissioned ranks in the three services; each rank is shown opposite to its equivalent in the other service:

The Armed Forces symbolise the unity of the country and the ideals of national integration. Recruitment to the Armed Forces is open to all Indian nationals, irrespective of caste, creed, community, religion and region. The endeavour has been to provide free and equal opportunities to all sections of the population to join the Armed Forces and render service in accordance with the ideals of secularism, democracy and social justice. India's Armed Forces offer challenging openings to our youth. A remarkable feature of recruitment to the Armed Forces is that it is entirely voluntary. The competition for entry into the service is intense, reflective of the increasing numbers of educated youth in the country, coupled with the attractive terms and conditions of service, and the high level of respect commanded by the Armed Forces. Recruitment is made from different states/union territories on the basis of their recruitable male population. Conscious efforts are made to take care of the special needs of the border areas and hilly and other remote areas, by lowering educational and certain other criteria to suit their requirements.

While provision has all along existed for women to join the Armed Forces Medical Services, the Armed Forces Dental Services and the Military Nursing Service, Section 12 of the Army Act provided that women would not normally be eligible for enrolment in the Army. Similar provisions also existed in the cases of the Air

Force and the Navy. However, in acknowledgment of the changing times, the Government has approved the induction of women into selected non-combatant branches in the three Forces. The entry of women has however, been restricted to the Officer Cadres, and they are on Short Service Commission basis. Further continuance of schemes would be decided on the basis of the experience gained. In pursance of this decision, several women officers have since joined the Service, in the EME, Signals, Engineers, Army Education Corps, Army Ordnance Corps, Army Service Corps and in the Judge Advocate General Department.

Entry to the Officer Cadres in the Armed Forces is primarily through the Union Public Service Commission (UPSC). Graduates are eligible to join the Armed Forces through an examination known as the Combined Defence Services Examination (CDSE) conducted by the UPSC twice a year. Candidates who quality in the examination join the Indian Military Academy (IMA), the Air Force Academy and the Naval Academy for pre-commission training. Individuals selected for Short Service Commission are trained at the Officers Training Academy. The candidates seeking a career in the Armed Forces after completion of 10+2 general education join the National Defence Academy (NDA). UPSC holds the entrance examination twice a year for entry in the NDA. They join the respective Service Academies viz. the Indian Military Academy (IMA) for the Army, the Air Force Academy for the Air Force and the Naval Academy for the Navy, for their pre-commission training.

There is also direct entry of officers through the Service Selection Boards (SSBs) for the Army and Navy, and through the Air Force Selection Board for the Air Force, without any written examination by the UPSC. Candidates in the age group of 20 to 27 years with Engineering Degree and Post-Graduates in specified subject in the age group of 23 to 27 years are eligible for interview by the respective Selection Boards of the following branches of the Armed Forces: Armed Engineers, Electrical and Mechanical Engineering, Signals, Army Education Corps, Military Farms, Remount and Veterinary Corps: Navy–Electrical and Engineering, Engineering (Naval Architects) Logistics, Law, Education, Air Traffic control: Air Force–Aeronautic Engineers (Electronics), Aeronautic Engineers (Mechanical), Administration, Education, Logistics, Accounts, Meteorology.

In July 1992, the Government approved a University Entry Scheme, initially for a period of three years, for induction of Engineering students in their final year/pre-final into the Army. This scheme is already operating in the Air Force and the Navy. Engineering students of various disciplines studying in the final/pre-final years in recognised universities/institutions are eligible for induction into the technical branches/services of the Army as short service commissioned officers with the rank of Second Lieutenants under this scheme. Their salary, however, is paid in one lump sum on their joining the IMA for training on the successful completion of which they will be granted permanent commission in the Army. An intake of 100 officers per year has been planned under this scheme.

With a view to mitigate the shortage of Technical Officers (Engineering) in the Army, the Government also approved a short service commission (Tech) Entry Scheme. This envisages recruitment of qualified technical graduates through the SSBs and their enrolment in the Officers' Training Academy (OTA), Madras after medical tests for a ten month course. At the end of the course, the successful candidates will receive short service commission. Thereafter, they will be governed by the rules applicable to the other short service commissioned officers.

Recruitment of medical officers in the Armed Forces is done through two sources. All MBBS graduates passing out from the Armed Forces Medical College, Pune are granted Permanent Commission. Apart from this, post graduates/MBBS degree holders passing out from civilian medical colleges are selected through competitive examinations, on an all-India basis, conducted by the Directorate General of Armed Forces, partyly for grant of Regular Commission and partly for grant of Short Service Commission.

In order to maintain a youthful profile of the Armed Forces, over 55,000 service personnel are retired/released every year at a comparatively young age. Majority of service personnel at the time of retirement are at an age where they have numerous unfinished responsibilities which necessitate their taking up of a second career. The Government is seized of this problem of rehabilitating them through provision of employment in organised sector or through self-employment. The welfare of ex-servicemen has been accepted as a national responsibility.

The Directorate General of Resettlement (DGR) under the Ministry of Defence (MOD) has been set up to look after all matters connected with resettlement and welfare of ex-servicemen and their dependents. A Kendriya Sainik Board under the Chairmanship of Raksha Mantri has been established for laying down general policy for the welfare of ex-servicemen and their dependents, for the administration of welfare funds, and also for coordinating the work of the Sainik Boards in the country. At the state level, the Rajya Sainik Boards, and at the district level the Zila Sainik Boards, have been established. The Government of India bears 50 per cent of the expenditure incurred on the organisations of Rajya and Zila Sainik Boards, the remaining expenditure is borne by the respective state governments.

Resettlement activities for the retired/retiring service personnel consist of the following:

— training programmes to reorient retiring Defence personnel towards civil emploment;

— providing re-employment opportunities in government/semi-government/public sector organisations and

— schemes for self-employment.

In order to equip retiring service personnel for employment, suitable training programmes have been devised. They equip them for employment in civil organisations and for self-employment. For retiring service officers, the following training programmes were introduced during 1994-95:

— Diploma in Industrial Security and Labour Laws;

— Coaching for Air Line Transport Pilot Licence/Senior Commercial Pilot Licence/Commercial Helicopter Pilot Licence;

— Consultant in ISO-9000;

— Quality Assurance Manager ISO-9000 and

— Deputy Quality Assurance Manager ISO-9000.

Up to March 1995, 882 officers were trained. The vocational training, ITI training and on the job training are presently being conducted for retiring Service personnel other than officers.

Re-employment constitutes a major means of rehabilitation of ex-servicemen. To achieve this goal both the Central and state governments have provided various concessions/facilities. These include reservation of posts, relaxations in age/educational standards, priority in employment etc. The Central Government has reserved 10 per cent of Group 'C' and 20 per cent of Group 'D' posts for ex-servicemen in Central ministries/ departments. The percentage of reservation in public sector undertakings and nationalised banks in these are 14½ and 24½ per cent respectively. Besides, there is 10 per cent reservation for the post of Assistant Commandants in para-military Forces. Reservation under the state governments varies from two per cent to 20 per cent. There is no reservation for ex-servicemen in Bihar, Kerala and Megahalaya.

DGR has been nominating ex-servicemen security agencies to various PSUs and private sector organisations. These security agencies provide employment opportunities for officers and other ranks. There are over 173 ex-servicemen security agencies which are registered with DGR, of which 130 have been sponsored for work. This alone has generated employment opportunities for over 6,419 ex-servicemen and over 250 officers.

There is considerable scope for absorption of ex-servicemen in para-military forces like CRPF, BSF, ITBP, CISF, etc. However, the response of ex-servicemen for joining these forces has been generally poor. With a view to achieve fuller utilisation of reserved vacancies, special recruitment rallies were organised in selected states. During 1993, special recruitment drives were conducted by CISF.

The concept of Ecological Task Force was mooted in 1992 for the purpose of restoring the forest cover in regions where significant deforestation had taken place. These units were initially raised in three states viz., Uttar Prasdesh, Rajasthan and J&K. The task forces are manned by ex-servicemen who are paid salaries as per TA scales. Every individual, irrespective of his rank prior to retirement, is re-employed as a sepoy. Ministry of Defence provides officers to command these units.

Important schemes for self employment for ex-servicemen are SEMFEX-I, SEMFEX-II and SEMFEX-III. These schemes have been launched in collaboration with the Small Industries Development Bank of India, NABARD and the Khadi and Village Industries Commission for providing extensive self-employment opportunities for ex-servicemen and their dependents.

The SEMFEX-I Scheme was launched in April, 1987. Under this Scheme, financial assistance is provided to ex-servicemen to set up small industrial projects for self-employment. Loans under this Scheme are provided by the respective State Financial Corporation. As on 31 December 1994 there were 6,686 beneficiaries and the amount sanctioned is to the tune of Rs. 179.27 crore since inception.

The SEMFEX-II Scheme was launched in January 1988 by the DGR in collaboration with the National Bank for Agricultural and Rural Development (NABARD) to provide assistance for agricultural and allied activities. Under the Scheme, financial assistance up to Rs. 7.5 lakh for setting up of industrial units/service establishments is given. The ceiling of Rs. 7.5 lakh is, however, not applicable for setting up of units relating to agro-industries. Since inception and up to December 1994 loans amounting to Rs. 12.30 crore have been sanctioned to 2,352 beneficiaries.

The SEMFEX-III Scheme was launched in October 1991 in collaboration with the Khadi and Village Industries Commission (KVIC). It provides self employment opportunities for setting up village industries under the purview of KVIC. Under this Scheme, ex-servicemen and their widows are eligible to take up self-employment ventures. Financial assistance for such ventures is provided under a liberalised pattern of assistance by the KVIC. The loans granted to village industries under this Scheme carry a rate of interest of four per cent and there is no interest on loan for Khadi units. The Scheme is picking up. Up to December 1994, a loan of Rs. 1.42 crore was sanctioned in 188 cases.

Schemes have also been launched in collaboration with Bombay Mercantile Cooperative Bank and Oriental Bank of Commerce to provide financial assistance to ex-servicemen and their widows on easy terms. In addition to the above schemes for financial assistance, certain other measures have also been taken to assist ex-servicemen in their self employment ventures. These are: (a) Allotment of sheds/plots; (b) Price subsidy to ex-servicemen units; (c) Allotment of surplus class V-B vehicles; (d) Allotment of repairable typewriters and duplicators; (e) Transportation of bulk LPG; (f) Allotment of Mother Dairy milk booths, fruit and vegetable outlets; (g) Transportation of coal and (h) Allotment of petroleum product agencies.

Before April, 1993 there were four separate funds viz., amalgamated Special Fund for War Bereaved, War Disabled and other ex-Servicemen/serving personnel; (i) Flag Day Fund; (ii) ST Dunstan's (India) and KSB Fund and (iv) Indian Gorkha Ex-Servicemen's Welfare Fund. These separate funds have been merged into an 'Armed Forces Flag Day Fund'.

The Kendriya Sainik Board (KSB) administers 'Armed Forces Flag Day Fund' for the welfare and rehabilitation of ex-servicemen, war widows, disabled service personnel and their dependents. The total corpus of the fund, as on 31 March 1995 was Rs. 45.60 crore. The corpus of the fund is invested with Banks/PSUs. The income accruing from interest is utilised for the various welfare activities. In the year 1994-95, Rs. 2.20 crore were spent on the major welfare activities. Financial assistance is also provided to institutions such as Paraplegic Homes at Kirkee and Mohali, Cheshire Homes, Military Hospitals, St. Dunstan After Care Organisations and Homes for taking care or old and physically handicapped ex-servicemen and their dependents. Financial assistance is also provided to individual ex-servicemen suffering from serious diseases for treatment in civil hospitals in case they cannot be treated in Military Hospitals and have not availed similar assistance from any other source. During 1994-95, a sum of Rs. 20,59,719.60 was sanctioned for the treatment of serious diseases.

To collect reliable data about ex-servicemen/widows population and update it on a regular basis a census of ex-servicemen is being carried out by DGR through Zila Sainik Boards (ZSBs) with effect from 15 May 1992. The Scheme envisages registration of retired defence service personnel with their ZSBs and issue of I-cards to the eligible ex-servicemen/widows. As per the feedback received, a total of 12.01 lakh ex-servicemen and 2.06 lakh widows have been registered and were reported to be surviving as on 31 December 1994.

The Government has been granting various concessions to ex-servicemen from time to time. The major concessions granted to different categories of personnel or their dependents cover assistance in the field of education, reservation for wards in professional institutions, reservations in Sainik Schools and Military Schools, medical treatment, assistance for construction/ repair of houses, financial assistance for the marriage of daughters, canteen facilities, rail and air travel concessions. Besides, financial assistance from the Raksha Mantri's Discretionary Fund (RMDF) is given to old and infirm exservicemen and to their widows in indegent circumstances.

The revised rates of financial assistance are: (a) Assistance to old infirm ex-servicemen/widows of ex-servicemen Rs. 250 per month for two years; (b) Marriage of daughters of ex-servicemen/widows in penury Rs. 4000; (c) Repair of house for ex-servicemen/widows in penury Rs. 5,000; (d) Medical treatment-depending upon the nature and gravity of ailment subject to a maximum of Rs. 8,000; (e) Education of children of ex-servicemen/ widows in penury Rs. 35 per month per child for up to three children up to class X and (f) Other cases in respect of ex-servicemen/widows in penury (like natural calamities, accidental death or where RM/RRM feel that the case deserves sysmpathetic consideration–no single transaction to exceed Rs. 8,000.

In pursuance of the recommendation of the high level empowered committee headed by the Raksha Mantri on improvement in the retirement pensions of Defence Personnel, the Ministry of Defence constituted an Inter-Ministerial Committee to deal with the problems of ex-servicemen other than those relating to pensionary matters. Accordingly, a committe under the chairmanship of an Additional Secretary in the Ministry of Defence was set up. This committee included representatives from the Ministry of Finance, Ministry of Law, Department of Pension and Pension and Pensioners' Welfare and other relevant organisations. The Committee considered 53 demands of ex-servcemen. It has recommended/partly recommended 33 demands, noted that five demands were not found justified. The demands which have already been accepted by Government are: (i) Permission for commercial employment after retirement; (ii) Provision of Soft Seed Capital Assistance under SEMFEX-II Scheme; (iii) Non-allotment of oil production agencies to ex-servicemen/widows; (iv) Reservation in purchase from ex-servicemen entrepreneurs; and (v) Issue of Last Pay Certificate along with discharge certificate.

A substantial part of defence stores needed by the Services is now being developed and produced within the country. The responsibility for this has been entrusted to the Department of Defence Production and Supplies in the Ministry of Defence. The Department directs and coordinates production of material and equipment required by the Armed Forces.

At present, 39 ordnance factories spread all over India operate a wide-range of technologies and product mix. Some of the important products are field guns, anti-aircraft guns, mortars, various small arms and ammunition for weapons and guns, rockets, projectiles, pyro-technics, bombs, grenades, mines, demolition charges, depth charges, infantry combat vehicles, battle tanks, self-propelled guns, transport trucks and petrol vehicles, high-altitude and combat clothing, optical and fire control instruments, engineering equipment, supply dropping equipmet including parachutes, rubberised items, various knitted and woven items like blankets, web equipment and a wide range of general stores are produced by them. Production of 5.56 mm (indigenously designed) weapon system has started in ordnance factories. These factories are also producing bombs required by Air Force. Besides, liquid fuel required for successful flight trials of Prithvi and Agni missiles, igniters and copper liners for the warheads were also supplied in the development of Prithvi missile. The production of Ajeya tank (T-72), Sarath (BMP-II), infantry combat vehicle are carried out at Heavy Vehicle Factory, Avadi and Ordnance Factory, Medak, respectively. A sophisticated opto-electronic production unit has been set up at Dehra Dun to produce the opto-electronic fire control and night vision devices required for Ajeya Tank (T-72-MI and Sarath* infantry combat vehicle is planned from 1994-95. To utilise the sparable capacities, after meeting the services requirements, linear and lateral shift in customer product profiles has been taken up as a major thrust area of operations.

As a part of diversification efforts, Vehicles Factory, Jabalpur (VFJ) has taken up modification and upgradation of Jonga. The vehicle, conforming to military standards, is not only sturdy but also has a very high pick up, high fuel efficiency of 16 km per litre (under test conditions) and a maximum speed of 120 kmph with gradient climbing capability of one in three. It has been decided to launch Jonga in the civil open market. VFJ has a captive capacity to manufacture 20,000 Jonga per annum. Out of this, 10,000 vehicles are to be released in the civil market and remaining 10,000 are reserved for the Army and exports. The release to the civil market would be done without effecting any erosion in the Army requirements.

There are eight public sector undertakings (PSUs) under the Department of Defence Production and Suppliers. These are: Hindustan Aeronautics Limited (HAL), Bharat Electronics Limited (BEL), Bharat Earth Movers* rail coaches, track laying equipments, heavy duty trucks, trailers, diesel engines etc. BEML is a leader in earth-moving industry with over 70 per cent market share. Its equipments and systems are productively deployed in India and over 30 other countries across the globe.

Mazagon Dock Limited (MDL) is the country's leading shipbuilding yard and can build warships up to 6,000 DWT displacement and merchant ships up to 27,000 DWT. It has units at Bombay, Nhava and Mangalore and headquarters at Bombay. At present, its major activities include construction of sub-marines, missile-boats and destroyers etc., for the Indian Navy and off-shore supply vessels and well-head platforms etc., for the Oil and Natural Gas Commission (ONGC). The company also provides diving services as well as services for coating/ laying sub-sea pipes.

Garden Reach Shipbuilders and Engineers Limited (GRSE) is a multi-unit shipyard-cum-general engineering company. It has six units in and around Calcutta and a Diesel Engine Plant at Ranchi (Bihar). Its corporate office is at Calcutta. It has three distinct divisions, namely, ship, engineering and engine divisions. It is presently engaged in the construction of war ships and auxiliary vessels of various types for the Navy and the Coast Guard and to undertake repair of vessels of these two organisations. Other products of the company include a variety of high technology ship-borne equipments, portable Bailey type steel bridges, marines sewage treatment plant, dock-machinery items, turbine pumps for the agricultural sector, diesel engines, etc.

The activities of Goa Shipyards Limited (GSL) located at Vasco-da-Gama, primarily comprise construction and repair-reit of ships/vessels. It has undertaken construction/refit of variety of vessels for the Indian Navy and the Coast Guard as well as for the non-defence sector. It is currently building advanced off-shore patrol vessels of in-house design.

Bharat Dynamics Limited (BDL), established in 1970, is primarily engaged in the manufacture of guided missiles and allied equipments. It has units at Hyderabad and Bhanur (Medak district). Its corporate office is at Hyderabad. It is also the prime production agency for manufacture of four new missile systems, namely, Prithvi, Trishul, Akash and Nag, being developed indigenously. Its activities which had earlier been diversified into a number of Naval projects now proposes to take up manufacture of small arms required for para-military forces of the country.

Mishra Dhatu Nigam Limited (MIDHANI) located at Hyderabad was incorporated in 1973. MIDHANI's product range includes super alloys, maraging steels, heat resistance alloys, controlled expansion alloys, tungsten, molybednum etc., in variety of mill forms.

There are 12 Zonal Recruiting Officers (ZROs) and 58 Branch Recruiting Officers (BROs) spreasd throughout the country. In addition, there is an Independent Recruiting Office (IRO) at Delhi. In order to inform the potential candidates well in advance of the commencement of recruitment extensive recruitment publicity is undertaken throughout the country, including in remote areas. Recruitment rules provide for relaxation in respect of educational and physical standards to the candidates from certain specified backward, remote and tribal regions to give them due representation in the Army. Relaxation in physical standards is also given to one son and one grandson of serving soldiers, ex-servicemen, widows of battle casualties, etc. The recruitment to the Navy has been clubbed with Army from the beginning. The recruitment demand is projected to Army Headquarters by Naval Headquarters.

Recruitment of Airmen to the Indian Air Force is done through the Central Airmen Selection Board located at the Air Force Station, New Delhi. There are 13 selection centres under this Board and they make the necessary arrangements for the conduct of selection tests and final enrolment. After seeking the application through advertisements in national/regional dailies and through the mass media, a written test on an all-India basis is held and the all India merit list is drawn up with help of computers.

A Pilot Project has been undertaken for the direct recruitment of trained manpower from the civil stream in the trades, such as clerks, drives, and Surveyor Automated Cartography. Besides direct recruitment of technically qualified civilian personnel as JCO (Catering) has been introduced.

The National Cadet Corps (NCC) has emerged as the single largest structured youth movement in India. It was established on 15 July 1948. It has 11.5 lakh boys and girls in the Senior and Junior Divisions in the Army, Navy and Air Force Wings. This strength covers four per cent of the eligible student population in the country. NCC with motto 'Unity and Discipline' has following aims: (a) to develop qualities of character, courage, comradeship, leadership, secular outlook, spirit of adventure and sportsmanship and the ideal of selfless service among the youth to make them useful citizens; and (b) to create a human resource of organised, trained and motivated youth, to provide leadership in all walks of life including the Armed Forces and to be always available for the service of the nation.

Director General NCC located at New Delhi controls and oversees various activities of the NCC through 16 NCC Directorates spread across the country. There is a Central Advisory Committee for the NCC to provide overall policy guidelines. NCC is manned by Service personnel, whole time NCC officers and civilians. One lecturer/teacher in each educational institution is appointed as Associate NCC Officer.

During 1994-95, 21 centrally organised camps were held in which 5,575 cadets participated from Army, Navy, and Air and Girls Wings and 66 National Integration Camps were conducted across the country in which nearly 35,185 cadels have participated. A total of 3,65,151 cadets have attended Annual Training Camps till March 1995. One hundred and sixty girl cadets attached with Air Units attended the ATC at Belgaum and 160 girls attached with Naval Units attended ATC at Visakhapatam. As many as 110 officers and 8,902 cadets participated in attachment training during the year, 853 girl cadets did attachment training with Armed Forces hospitals. Twenty boys and 20 girls did para basic courses at Agra during November-December 1994. Besides, 4,59,992 NCC cadets participated in social service activities such as blood donation, eye donation, Cheshire homes, anti-dowry pledge, adult education etc., and 6,45,369 saplings were planted.

A team of eight officers and 42 cadets (21 boys and 21 girls) visited Canada in July 1994 under Indo-Canada Youth Exchage Programme. A similarly composed Canadian contingent was in India till January 1995. While 57 cadets visited other foreign countries on a reciprocal Youth Exchange Programme and one officer from Singapore and 32 foreign cadets from seven countries attended the Republic Day Camp (NCC) 1995. During 1994-95, 48 NCC personnel were awarded DGNCC's Commendation Cards with badges for outstanding contribution to the organisation. Five RM's Commendation Cards with hadges and seven Defence Secretary's Commendation Cards were awarded to two NCC cadets and five officers.

Sainik schools prepare boys academically and physically for entry into National Defence Academy. There are 18 sainik schools in the country, one in each state, except in Nagaland, Meghalaya, Tripura, Sikkim, Arunachal Pradesh, Mizoram and Goa. These schools are affiliated to the Central Board of Secondary Education and follow the 10+2 pattern, in science stream.

Admission is made to class VI on the basis of an all-India entrance examination held every year in February, in which boys in the age group of 10-11 years are eligible to appear. From 1992-93 academic session lateral admission to class IX has also been started for which the boys have to be 13-14 years of age on 1st July of that year. Since its inception, a total of 4,647 boys from these schools were selected for admission to the National

Defence Academy, Naval Academy, Armed Forces Medical College etc.

The National Defence Academy (NDA), Khadakwasla, is a Joint Services Training Institution which imparts academic as well as service training. The NDA has been brought in step with the national education format of 10+2+3. The syllabus of the Academy was reviewed to meet these requirements and has been approved by the Jawaharlal Nehru University for the grant of BA/B.Sc degree, at the time of passing out from Academy. the first course commenced training on revised syllabi in January 1989. After passing out from the NDA, the cadets go to their respective service acadmies for further training before being commissioned as officers in the Armed Forces. The present authorised training strength of the Army, Navy and Air Force cadets at the Academy is 1,800. This includes cadets from Bhutan and other friendly countries on as required basis.

The Indian Military Academy (IMA), Dehra Dun caters for training of cadets for commission into the Army. Cadets join the Indian Military Academy as per the following modes of entry: (a) on passing out from NDA, (b) on graduation from the Army Cadet College which is a wing of the IMA itself, (c) Direct entry graduate cadets who join on qualifying at the Union Public Service Commission Examination and the Services Selection Board, and (d) Technical graduates and University Entry Scheme. The present authorised strength of trainees at the IMA is 1,200 which includes cadets from Bhutan, Shri Lanka, Maldives, Mauritius and Nepal. The authorised training strength of Army Cadet College is 450.

The Officers Training Academy (OTA), Madras imparts pre-commission training for the following type of courses, (a) Short Service Commission Course of 44 weeks for university graduates who quality in the Union Public Service Commission; (b) course of six months for lady cadets (Women Special Entry Scheme); (c) Permanent Commission on Special List (PC) (SL) to selected service candidates, who qualify after a training of four weeks and (d) Regimental Commission Course for selected service candidates, who qualify after a training of 13 weeks duration. Authorised training strength of the Academy is 500. So far 50 lady cadets have been granted Short Service Commission.

Education on public school lines is imparted at the Rashtriya Indian Military College (RIMC), Dehradun principally for the boys who subsequently desire to join the NDA with a view to obtaining a commission in the Armed Forces. The College runs classes from eighth to 10+2 class. Selection for the RIMC is through a written examination cum viva voce conducted through the state governments. Seats for the respective states are reserved, based on population. Intake into the RIMC is bi-annual.

Inaugurated by Pandit Nehru in 1960, the National Defence College is an Inter-Service Organisation functioning under the Ministry of Defence. The NDC is the highest defence institution in India imparting instructions on all elements of national security and strategy to officers due to become Major Generals and equivalent and attain similar status in the Civil Service. The aim is to equip these policy makers with the necessary background and understanding of the total system of economic, political, military, scientific, international relations, national organisational aspects and the planning necessary for national security, both in its internal dynamics as well as the external comulsions. The head of the College is the Commandant, with five faculty members from the Army, Navy, Air Force, IAS, IFS and an administrative staff.

Army Cadet College is a Wing of IMA which caters for the training of service cadets selected for commission. The academic format is similar to the NDA on the lines of 10+2+3, and the syllabus is common. On completion of the course these cadets also qualify for a BA/BSc degree recognised by the Jawaharlal Nehra University.

The College of Combat, Mhow conducts the higher command, senior command and junior command courses for Army officers. It also conducts a Combined Operational Review and Evaluation (CORE) programme for selected senior officers of the rank of Major General and equivalent of the three Services once every year. College of Military Engineering, Kirkee (Pune), imparts training to the officers and other ranks in all aspects of military engineering. Long courses of over two years duration are also conducted to train officers up to degree standards. Military College of Telecommunication Engineering, Mhow imparts basic and advanced technical training in telecommunications and signal tactics. Armoured Corps Centre and School, Ahmednagar, conducts training in tactical handling of armoured fighting vehicles, driving and maintenance. School of Artillery, Deolali, provides training in field branch artillery. The Air Defence Guided Missiles School at Gopalpuron-sea trains personnel of the Air Defence Artillery. The High Altitude Warfare School located at Gulmarg and Sonmarg train personnel in the art of mountain warfare including rock, snow and ice-craft. The Counter Insurgency and General Warfare School, Viairengate, trains officers and men in the art of combating insurgency.

Mechanised Infantry Regimental Centre conducts basic and technical training for recruits of mechanised infantry. In addition, it runs basic and instructor courses on anti-tank guided missiles for officers, JCOs and other ranks of mechanised infantry. It also carries out conversion training of units when they are converted to mechanised infantry or when change in equipment is involved. College of Materials Management, Jabalpur, imparts specialised training in materials management including ammunition and explosives and also in contemporary materials management techniques. Some of the other Army training centres and schools are Army Service Corps School, Bareilly; EME School, Vadodara; Military College of Electronics and Mechanical Engineering, Secunderabad; College of Defence Management, Secunderabad; Remount and Veterinary Corps Centre and School, Meerut; Army Eucation Corps Training College and Centre, Pachmari; Army School Physical Training, Pune; Army/Air Transport School, Agra; Military Intelligence Training School and Depot, Pune; Army School of Mechanical Transport, Bangalore; Corps of Military Police Centre and School, Bangalore; Institute of Military Law, Kamptee; Armed Forces Medical College Pune; Institute of National Integration, Pune and Army Medical Corps Centre and School, Lucknow.

In talking of operational capability, one must remember with pride, the magnificent contribution by our network of Ordnance Factories which produce almost every weapons system and ammunition used by the three services. What is needed now is a large—scale induction of the latest technology from abroad to meet the specific requirements of the latest acquisitions in the three services. Equally in place is the well deserved tribute to the vast Research and Development activities under the umbrella of DRDO. No doubt, the latest INSAS Rifles systems may have its drawbacks, but as has been rightly pointed out by Ordnance experts there is imperative need for acquiring requisite technology from abroad for improving its design since such guns are already in use in USA and Austria.

India can be proud of its IMDP (Integrated Missile Development Programme) which has now after more than two decades produced four missiles with varied applications-Prithvi, Akash, Trishul and Nag. This family meets the requirements of multifaceted attack and defensive modes. But the crowing glory of defence research has been its development of the Intermediate Range Balistic Missile, the Agni with its range upto 2500, depending on the load.

The entire missile programme barring the Agni, is on the threshold of the production stage and it is here in this context that the defence sector undertakings such as Bharat Dynamics, the nodal agency, the HAL, Bharat Electronics and Bharat Earth Movers Ltd. are putting in integrated efforts to speed up the final fabrication stage. This missile programme has been well designed to meet the needs of all the three services. The Prithvi and the Nag for the Army and Akash and Trishul for the Air force. Both the Prithvi and Trishul can be modified or optimised for use by the Navy for surface to surface firing and surface skimming offensive power respectively.

The thrust of this presentation is also to focus attention to essential factors if not more on defence preparedness.

We must realise that Policy Planning and Strategy on a macro level are more important than additions to weapons, manpower or support systems.

It is in this context one must have Perspective Planning over an extended period of anywhere between five to twenty years. In other words our outlook has to undergo radical change as we have been doing in the field of build up of economic infrastructure in our country. We have taken a very bold step, infact a revolutionary one, in striking a balance between public ownership and control to a liberalised economy throwing open vast avenues of business and industry not only to private sector in India but to direct investment from abroad.

Keeping this in mind we have to evolve a policy of an open door approach and access to the defence sector establishments including Ordnance Factories, both in terms of exports, and induction of technology. The present day policy of outmoded secrecy for the sake of secrecy is a fallacy because whenever imports are made from abroad the seller invariably comes to know what we are doing or plan to do.

The mention of this factor has become imperative because of abnormally slow rate of progress by the defence sector undertaking at Bolangir in Orissa for manufacture of critical ammunition for medium and light guns. This project has been bogged down in controversy. This is a classic case of where defence preparedness has suffered due to lack of coherent policy planning.

This is only a tip of the iceberg. Having dragged our feet on a full production line for the T-72M tanks, it has now been decided as a matter of policy to acquire off the shelf these tanks of advanced versions and also secure technology for their production in India. Infact, as a matter of wrong policy the manufacture of T-72 was stalled with unwarranted claims of imminent productionisation of Indian Arjun MBT.